The Best is Yet to Come!

Proceeds from the sale of this book shall go to the not-for-profit Winspiration Day Association in order to disseminate the idea of the Winspiration Day and the Human Rights Development Index.

Writing:
Gabriele Borgmann, www.raum-zeichen.de

Cover illustrations, Winspiration Day logo:
Simon Hofer, www.simonhofer.ch

Translation:
Mary McCusker, USA

Editor:
Romana Vlcek, Australia

ed. 005

Wolfgang Sonnenburg

The Best is Yet to Come!

„What the caterpillar calls the end of the world,
the rest of the world calls a butterfly."

Lao Tzu

Contents

Foreword by Pero Mićić

Would you want to live in the year 1900 rather than today? During the time of the German Empire? With a six-day working week of 60 hours for all? Without suffrage for women? When ten percent of mankind was still dying from tuberculosis?

Sometimes one has the feeling that everything was much better in the early days. But if you examine this more closely, hardly anyone would want to dispense with the current quality of life. On the whole we are much better off now than twenty or a hundred years ago.

There is also a down side – complexity and excessive demand everywhere. A climate disaster around the corner. When the oil crisis took place in 1973, everyone thought it would be downhill from there. Rivers were already polluted. Nuclear war was only a question of time. But things turned out differently. Better. We have improved a few things.

Will the future too be better than our presence? Is the best yet to come? If you have doubts, I understand you. People are as always short-term beings. We sacrifice our better future too often in order to feel good now. Debt crises, environmental destruction, hunger, obesity and lack of qualifications are only a few examples of the fatal consequences of our short-term orientation. Our reward system in our brains was created over a period of millions of years. Thousands of years ago we did not have to worry about the future. This is why it is so difficult to do the right thing for tomorrow. We are overly challenged by complexity.

But there are grounds for cautious optimism. We have better resources today and a better understanding of the world. Step by
step we will also master the threatening and seemingly insoluble
problems of our time.

In order to do so we need a good relationship to our „Future I"
and our „Future We". We must measure our current thinking and
action against whether it will have beneficial or adverse effects on
the happiness of our Future I.

Will we have even greater affluence? This is a central goal in the
under-developed regions of this world. The greatest needs disappear once material prosperity has been achieved. But we don't
need more wealth in the literally saturated societies of the developed world. We yearn for a greater quality of life. This is what
should and will be growing, without foreseeable boundaries.

Wolfgang Sonnenburg combines freedom and responsibility, this
inseparable pair of values, in his own personality. He has taken his
freedom and is assuming his responsibility. This book allows one
to experience Winspiration in another form.

What can you do? What can we all do? Always look at the whole of
life and not just the moment. Learn how to know and love our Future I. Learn how to know and love our Future We. Always reflect
on the long-term consequences of our actions. Look longer and
harder at the whole rather than at ourselves.

Then it will be true: the best is yet to come.

Greeting by Samy Molcho

When Wolfgang first invited me to his Winspiration Day, I thought: oh, another motivation event! This was very popular in Germany at the time.

I was very surprised to experience something completely different than I had expected: the presentations were different, the atmosphere in the hall was different, the enthusiasm was different. It was clearly Wolfgang who had understood how to define and implement the difference between motivation and inspiration.

Motivating someone assumes that the person doesn't feel like doing anything, but one should nevertheless motivate him or her – often with some sort of reward system.

Inspiration is something else. It is a spiritual power of creation, an invisible creative power, which is in each and every one of us.

Wolfgang has acknowledged people again and again during Winspiration Day, who have been successful due to their internal power and vision, despite physical or other limitations. These people have stood on the stage and have showed us what is possible if one only believes.

Our visions are realized if we engage our own power, if we reflect on what we can really do well.

Dear Wolfgang, I hope you find many readers who say: "I want to join in."

The gift that Wolfgang gives us all with this day is to ignite a fire in us, to awaken the courage and strength to realize our visions. Dreams should not remain dreams – they should become reality.

Thank you.

Introduction –
Thinking ahead

Three words were enough to galvanize a whole nation. Three words that became a synonym for inspiration, because they inspired people and gave them hope in a future full of opportunities: "Yes, we can." After being elected 44th President of the United States, Barack Obama stepped on stage and fulfilled a dream that Martin Luther King had once painted for the future. Sometimes dreams need 40 years or more to come true. Then they open horizons and happiness rains down. This proves to me that the power of thought, the belief in justice and a good future will dominate over time.

Many years ago I sallied forth to look for happiness. I talked to philosophers, natural scientists, to clergy of various religions. I listened to politicians and allowed the life stories of impressive people to influence me. And always the ultimate insight was that happiness consists of an abundance of knowledge and freedom, of the will to make the best of this life. If the political framework conditions are right, if all facets of human rights are guaranteed, a large space opens up for this timorous feeling of happiness. I would like to add another value to these criteria – vision. It gives us the strength to believe in our capabilities, because it promises us in only three words: "Yes, we can."

I want to invite you to play with the idea that the United Nations has published a report for over 20 years in which it asks: How does one measure human happiness? The architects of this model believe it is with the values of education, health, life expectancy and financial security. I am fascinated by this attempt to explain happiness across borders, because it places people in the center. It shows that happiness has many faces and is significantly more than a mathematical formula.

Push your doubts and old doctrines aside for once. Open your thoughts to the idea that every human being possesses very special and individual capabilities – from the day they are born onwards. Our task is to discover these capabilities, to safeguard them as a valuable treasure, in order to be able to say at the end of our life: I was happy.

I know that there will be critics who ask: "Where will we end up, if everyone does what they want?" I answer with a smile: "Very far. Farther than we can imagine today."

We live in a democracy that allows self-fulfillment and is open to individual ways of life. Never before has the world been so close together, thanks to modern technology and an understanding for art and cultures. Never before have there been so many opportunities to build one's own paths. So what is keeping us from approaching our goals with a light step? Why don't we look for those tasks that make our hearts beat faster and fire our imaginations?

Probably there will always be people on this planet who bash each other's heads in, who behave unfairly and who injure others for base reasons. Laws cannot prevent, only punish, this. These realities, too, are part of life. But should we stop, therefore, and deviate even a single millimeter from our own dreams, from dreams that allow us to grow beyond ourselves like lovers do? I don't think so.

We need people who can exert their own power, who can discover their capabilities and enrich the world. We can bring about many things, both large and small. Everyone can be an ambassador for happiness and satisfaction. That is what this book is about.

Engage in the vision of the Winspiration Day on the next few pages. People throughout the world celebrate this day on the 7th of May. I would like to encourage you to take the plan for your own happiness in hand and work on it – at major events, at vision parties or in a small group of friends. I invite you to learn more about my type of inspiration in the next few pages. I will recount minor episodes from the past ten years and an overall picture of this day, which can bring about so much, if people consolidate their energies, will form in your mind.

A year ago I founded a not-for-profit association in Zurich with a team in order to give this day even greater significance, to make it a set day in the calendar similar to Valentine's Day. The time was ripe to write this book. It became an inspirational book. At times reflective, at times personal, at times polarizing.

I am also publishing this book in order to attract you as a member of this association and ask you for donations, so that we can spread the idea of Winspiration Days around the world together. A single person can only do so much, but many people together can improve this world quite a bit. Many people together can give happiness in society larger, more important space, by for instance asking politicians to give more attention to the wonderful idea of the Human Development Index. Not gross domestic product, but human growth, is central. The focus is on soft values: education, health, freedom to style one's own life. In my opinion – in total they are a guarantee for happiness. Politicians should read the annual report of the United Nations and put it on their desks as a working document. They should leaf through it until the corners are dog-eared and consider how these values can constantly fit into their thoughts, actions and programs. At the same time I would like certain entrepreneurs to gain a greater awareness of the happiness of their employees, most teachers to have a broader view of their pupils' talents, parents to attend to their children with benevolence. I have written this book for all of them. I want to provide stimuli for ideas as part of the daily routine and once a year for concentration on what really counts in life.

I am really proud that the personalities that I was privileged to encounter are speaking out. They have all achieved great things. Such as Pero Mićić, Samy Molcho, Muhammad Yunus, Manfred Spitzer, Felix Finkbeiner, such as Joana Zimmer, Dagmar Riedel-Breidenstein and all those who impress me again and again. Because they spread their knowledge and passion and simply say: "Yes, I do."

Yours,

Wolfgang Sonnenburg

The Idea –
Getting back to basics

Just imagine- if the prosperity of a country would not be measured by its balance sheets alone? What would it be like, if people were not consumed by a crisis phobia; instead, their hearts were filled with hope for the future?

Wouldn't there be spontaneous constructive growth and more justice in this world?

It is already 20 years since the United Nations has been trying to broaden the national standards by encompassing education, health and happiness levels. It has declared way back in1990:

> "People are the real wealth of a nation. The basic objective of development is to create an enabling environment for people to enjoy long, healthy, creative lives. This may appear to be a simple truth. But it is often forgotten in the immediate concern with the accumulation of commodities and financial wealth." (From HDI, Objective 5)

The Winspiration Day Association supports this objective of the United Nations. It organizes an annual one day event to comprehend this Human Development Index as a personal opportunity. The index is aimed at bringing people together, encouraging them to follow their own path and breaking free from the shackles of old and limiting beliefs. This day must enable each person to create a plan of happiness for life. Imagine the tremendous energy that would be created if people all over the world participated in this endeavor! The Winspiration Day is celebrated on 7th May on stages, in homes, on the internet. It shall fire your dreams, ignite your visions. It shall touch people's hearts and exponentiate a million times to massive power.

Baden-Baden, 2006. The sun is shining over the white rocks. At last, you are beginning to experience a whiff of the impending summer. It is the day on which I have sent out invitations for a fourth time for Winspiration- a formidable agenda has been outlined this year. The press has already covered it. I was interviewed in the run-up. Everything has fallen into place exactly the way any facilitator wants it to be. Now I am standing in this empty, elaborate hall at the Baden-Baden resort. All alone. I am slightly nervous. But then, some nervousness is as native to a speaker as the tinkling of champagne glasses at twilight, when the curtains are drawn. I throw a glance outside. Colorful flowers grow hazy in front of my eyes, and I start to visualize the images from Yokohama. It was in this big Japanese town just a few weeks back that I got acquainted with little Rex. And this encounter moved me to the depth of my soul. This young boy entered the world nine years back with a major disability. He could not see, could not hear; he could hardly move. And it was evident in the first few years of his life itself: Little Rex was autistic as well. But he had one talent. His mother discovered his talent and nurtured it with immense love and devotion: Rex can play the piano. Just like that. He can memorize the compositions of the grand masters, and then recreate them. Without being able to read music. This gift seems to strengthen his hearing capability, improve his concentration, help him move better and fill his heart with joy. His disabilities seem to disappear into insignificance in the presence of melodies. He releases them to fly off to a faraway land. Until the last note slowly melts away. Rex represents very much what one would call a wonder child, the specia-

lists opine. But I call it his talent and hard work. He practices for hours, days, and loses himself in time and space. Tonight, I shall welcome him along with his mother to an audience of thousands of guests and award them the prize. I believe that this young boy has a message to spread. His mother captures it in her own words: "There is something hidden in each one of us. We all have our strengths. We all have our weaknesses. But if we are passionate about our vision, then we shall discover our unique abilities. Rex shall greet everyone with loud abandon in the hall: "Happy Winspiration Day!" No one has ever said that before. And me? I will probably turn towards the audience and ask them: "Rex plays the piano. And you?

http://may7.org/ugfe – Cathleen Lewis wrote the book: „Rex: A Mother, Her Autistic Child, and the Music that Transformed Their Lives".

The economic crisis as a value crisis

Close your eyes. Detach yourself from the outside world for a few minutes. Redirect your power for a moment towards yourself. Paint it in a light color and think of one single sentence: We have never been more prosperous.

How do you feel? Strange? Irritated? Well, this is normal. Most of us are programmed to complain, to fear, to hark back. We are susceptible to catastrophes. That was our grand evolutionary design: A flight response to danger was one of our biggest challenges. The brain has not yet forgotten these roadmaps and this is the very fact that is endearingly taken advantage of by the media: They dart for misfortune, dissect it till it reaches a painful threshold and then present it in a continuous loop; till the audience becomes insecure and turns away. Let us take the example of the incident that happened in the spring of 2007. Little Maddie disappeared. She had been with her parents on a holiday at a resort in Praia da Luz in Portugal. Till one evening, her parents found her room empty. They alarmed the police. Newspapers competed against each other to catch the reader's attention. For months, media exploited the fact that bad news give them better profits than good news. And in addition to this benefit, so to say, journalists also achieved something else that was more subtle and it slowly and stealthily made its way into the daily routine of the reader: A feeling of in-depth insecurity was created. Mothers started over-protecting their children, did not trust them to go to school on their own anymore, and forbade them to play in the park with their friends. The negative messages were not forgotten after reading the last sentence; instead, they assumed even greater proportions in their minds and feelings. There was an urgent need to catch hold of the culprit to finally end this drama and return to a routine sans worry.

Journalists did realize how the readers seemed to have lost their balance; in spite of this, they blatantly continued with their speculations. Their coverage created an image of an enslaved, dangerous period in time; as if children were being kidnapped in this manner all the time. This negative reporting distorted the contours of reality; and reality was that actually, life has indeed become safer and better for many years. It is highly probable that, at the same time and in parallel to that dreadful event, a mother has given birth to a healthy child, an adolescent has just completed his degree with the best mark, a surgeon has saved a life by operation, a company has averted insolvency, nations have signed a convention against violence for conflict prevention, a head of a state has released innocent prisoners by amnesty. The criteria of the millennium contract have probably been fulfilled to a larger extent. But yet the headlines report about track hounds in Portugal and talks of Maddie's parents with the press and the pope. And thus created further sadness and fear.

Responsibility instead of apathy

We have the media that we deserve. As long as vapid and parasitical C- and D-list reality show celebrities make more money than a road worker who slaves away with bent back for himself and the community, more than an intense care nurse who provides care for the ill, apathy will keep drifting through the country and there will be a lack of enriching life models. People need stimuli rather than dullness and apathy at the microlevel.

We live in a society where we leave imprints on our behavior when we nourish our minds with an abundance of bad news. But the issues and the tonality can be changed simply if the individual corrected his attitude by adopting the approach of facing reality with optimism. Our thoughts influence our actions; so is it any wonder then how insidiously our values are altered when hope dies and fear grows?

Fear makes for a bad counsellor

However, it would be unfair to blame only the politicians and media for people's fear of the future. It's not the media that invents bleak scenarios, nor only the politicians that create the problems; rather, it is every individual that affects the mood of the country. Each adult may elect his own political representatives, can bring issues to the legislature, can make requests and become involved. Everyone is responsible for morality. No single person should be told how to live it. If a person in office is accused of personal gain and his reputation is ruined even before a judge can pronounce a judgment, if the quota come before a person's right to protection of privacy and this person does not know how he is ever to regain a foothold in his life, then I believe that it is shameful; and on the other hand, it is an indication of how volatile morality can be. Christian Wulff [once German President from 2010-2012] was once celebrated as a glamorous political star. Then he fell in disgrace before the sensationalist media. Rarely have I seen a person age faster. How power slips away when one's personal space becomes the central stage for a tragedy.

I am sure that we can achieve much if we can avoid such situations. We should reflect on our strengths and on the purpose of making the best out of this life, beyond complaints and malice.

What if we provide an impetus on one day of the year to reach our goals and to fulfill our desires? What if we declared a special day in the year, dedicated to our life plan, as a holiday?

We would sense our potential. Together with others, with family, friends, colleagues, neighbors, we would reflect upon where our strengths lie and how we could use them. I know from many encounters, from lectures, discussions and coaching sessions, and from ten years of Winspiration Day, how strong this force can be. You can reduce or even eliminate poverty, allow wealth and happiness as well. If we enumerate what we want, when we say it, write it down and place it in the middle of the room, then it can grow into our lives and into the world.

The future of our children

What we need is positive thoughts for our future. To form them, we must very deliberately jump out of the rat race and say yes to moments beyond our careers or everyday duties. When was the last time you sat on the floor next to your child and built a tower out of blocks? When have you been out in nature jogging a lap, once again feeling that you have the oxygen to chase down the smallest pathways of the brain? When you have simply enjoyed a good laugh? When you have looked a man passing by in the eye and smiled at him? Each positive moment leaves a trail of happiness in our brain. Are you a collector of these precious little moments in everyday life?

We need moments of happiness, and sometimes, a more casual approach to life. We should find a balance between the major areas of finance, education and health, as described by the Human Development Index. Futurologists predict: Prosperity, as it has never existed before, is imminent. The promise of new technologies and new concepts of life; both will be game-changing. But we also need children to become confident, intelligent adults who will face the challenges of the future by acting responsibly, rather than just reacting as the teachers want them to. Creativity cannot be excluded by the closing of the classroom door. When teachers send children out to the hallway because they are interrupting lessons then nobody should be surprised that the little ones stand mute before authority. Such punishment belongs in a prior century; yet this is still being done at local primary schools. A more fitting educational approach should be according to the saying: "In the center stands the child with his creativity."

Children want to talk and not be silent. They want to discover their abilities, in their own way. They are not complacent and far from being tired of life. They take their future in hand, such as Felix Finkbeiner, who with his organization "Plants for the Planet" as a 12-year-old in 2007, called to plant trees to generate clean air. He spoke before the United Nations; he is the UN Child Ambassador for Climate Justice, and wrote the paper entitled "It's All Good – How Kids can Change the World". Today, the world is richer for his dedication to 12.6 billion trees. Winspiration Day once had him up on the stage and gave him an award.

120 years of life

He who speaks only when asked leaves no traces. He tiptoes through his time and submits to rules, rather than challenging them. One thing is certain: No one has infinite time, but everyone has the opportunity to use his own time well. More than two thousand years ago, Seneca said, "How long I live is not under my control; but whether I really live, while I live, depends upon me." And one fact is indisputable: We are living longer.

According to a recent OECD study, the average age of people in developed countries is 77 years. In Germany, the life expectancy is around 82 years. So we must think, feel and choose 82 times 31,536,000 seconds per year. And we are not far from living to 120 years or more; and thus to the sum of our life expectancy has increased by 50 percent. The prospects for a long and fulfilling life have never been better. They rise with the health, education and the happiness that everyone must feel when one remembers to make the most of one's life. Pessimists cry out, forecasting the writing on the wall, "For heaven's sake, who is supposed to pay for this? We are already stretched with the bailout for Europe; how will we even feed the old people?" I say, "Those who have learned to rely on their own skills, to design their lives with creativity and vision, shall independently prevent poverty in old age." New occupational and pension concepts will emerge. The retirement age is no longer limited to 65 years. Just 20 years ago men and women in their prime retired early at age 56. What a waste of knowledge resources and energy! Today politicians are calling for a retirement age of 67. We move forward in small steps.

Who keeps us from thinking big again, to toy with vision? Complaining makes the mind and body tired, and warps one's attitude to life. And it leaves traces in the brain that slowly but surely trample flat the views of the good. We must find alternatives to overcome the lack of courage; only this will generate flexibility for the future. Just think of the crisis scenarios of overpopulation in Europe in the recent past. They proved to be incorrect. Today, researchers predict that Europe's share of the world population at the end of 21st century will only be five to eight percent.

By the creation of crises, only one thing is achieved: fear. This never leads to growth and vitality. We should not allow ourselves to be like an uncontrolled ship on a stormy sea, left to the waves of media and pessimists. It seems much more sensible to me that a person should remember one's own responsibility with a good dose of self-confidence. Winspiration Day on May 7 is a day of focus. And with a bold look forward to every other day the insight may arise that: My goals are defined by me and not by the politicians, not by the media, the teacher, nor the boss, nor anyone else. The premise remains that you should do what you are passionate about, because this will lead to personal success and to the success of society. Already in the 12th century, Bernard of Clairvaux of the Holy Cisterian Order knew: "Passion is greater than knowledge."

Fate does not mean dispair

Since the first Winspiration Day in 2003, many other ones have followed in various formats. They are all shaped by people, who do something special, and by encounters you will never forget, such as the one with Jim McLaren.

I met Jim in a Starbucks Coffee Shop in Santa Fé. It was his eyes which captivated me. I saw this curiosity in his eyes, capturing each second of life around him. Among umpteen guests, I noticed the intensity of his charisma. Here was someone who looked extremely disabled. He was sitting in a wheelchair. His hands were so cramped that he could not even unscrew a bottle of mineral water. But everything about him certainly seemed to say yes to life. I watched him, and I quickly looked away again if he noticed. I drank my coffee more hastily than usual and left the shop earlier than usual. I stopped on the street and thought about it. "Why didn't I speak to this man? Why didn't I tell him how impressed I was by his aura? There arose within me the unpleasant sensation

of having missed the chance of a particularly special conver-
sation. I turned around, walked back, and it seemed as if he
had anticipated it. He nodded to me, and thus began our fri-
endship.

Jim McLaren was once a sport idol in the USA until he was struck by fate, until he was lamed from the cervical vertebrate downwards by two severe accidents. At the time I asked myself: How is that possible? How can I meet a man, who had been deprived of everything that had been important to him up until the tragic accidents – his agility, his speed and his fascination of sport – in a sensitive, life-affirming manner? The answer I found astonished me: Jim McLaren saw purpose in his fate by attempting to sharpen awareness in society for people with disabilities and to help them tangibly and mentally.

Jim's organization ensured that disabled men, women and children were no longer shunned worldwide. They received help. In his intelligent, quiet and self-confident manner, he fought to break down internal and external barriers. Owing to Jim McLaren, disabled people have a lobby, and they found a place in society and a new self-image. Development assistance should begin with the weak.

In 2006 I presented the Winspiration Award to Jim McLaren and 10,000 Euro for his foundation Choose Living. He commented on the award with words which splendidly describe the idea of the Winspiration Days: "People with the same desire got to know each other. They did not make a great plan to change the world. Instead, we want to reach and help individual people. You have helped me. I felt your energy – and I am not just saying that easily.

Who knows what the future has in store. I find it very exciting and thrilling. Thank you very much."

Jim McLaren died on August 31, 2010. Thank you Jim for your motivation in giving disabled people courage and a media response. Thank you for your words: "Being alive just means living. That is something good."

▌ http://may7.org/kqyu – Jim MacLaren (video)

Businesses need values

Minorities often lack media response, as journalists prefer to massage managing board egos at institutions and corporations, leaving much to be desired. Vanity and profit, however, cannot remain the sole motivators in the long run. People who work just to hoard money lose touch with the meaning of life and eventually end up in depression. Businesses that strive solely to issue invoices, but fail to observe quality standards, will not attain a good reputation in the long term. In his book, "Strategische Unternehmensführung" (Strategic Governance), Professor Hans Hinterhuber concludes that, all things considered, only companies that offer solutions for societal problems will have a future because, "People are more important than strategy." How very true!

It is not enough, if companies adopt mission statements merely for the sake of pretty words. Values become real only if employees can feel, breathe and share them. This happens when, meeting its responsibility, a company stimulates its employees, promotes their skills and gives them space for individual fulfillment and personal responsibility. This is a sure way to prevent individual burnout and collective collapse. It allows people to work on a higher plane, with joy resonating, because having a passion for a vision, inspired individuals can achieve truly great things. In this event, anxiety about the future, deprived of fertile ground, cannot thrive any longer.

Seeing the future

There is no reason for anxiety about the future. We are about to achieve a degree of prosperity, which we cannot even begin to imagine today. Futurologist, Mathias Horx, never tires of pointing out that we tend to harbor unjustified fears. To this day, students are reading in their textbooks that, due to an imminent global population boom, energy and food demand will be impossible to satisfy in future. On another note, let us recall a prophecy proclaimed loudly within esoteric circles about the end of the world coming in December 2012. Such unspeakable warning was derived solely from the fact that the Maya calendar would end at that point in time. Many an editor, toying with interpretation, set out to scaremonger and spread panic. Doomsday movies flooded the market. A gloating tourism industry made the most of it, maximizing holiday packages for Mexico, Guatemala and Honduras. And yet, to this day, the Earth is still moving.

In the Seventies, the energy crisis was worrying us. Car-free Sundays and mandatory driving at walking pace, when approaching a red light, were measures imposed to remedy the problem. However, the crisis never came. Scenarios have been drafted, where robots alone would perform surgery on humans. Yet, to this day, surgeons are performing the operations, while human relationships continue, and confidence in human ability prevails. On the other hand, the global village is closing ranks. Digital media provide information; denounce injustice and human rights violations that occur in the more remote parts of the world. New technologies are stepping up the pace. We cannot afford to blind ourselves to the fact. Rather, we would be well advised to educate ourselves and recognize the benefits of such new technologies.

Fifty years ago, it was absolute luxury to own a color TV set. Today, touch screens grace the walls of living rooms and eyeglasses feature chips that provide access to the virtual world at any time. Less than 180 years ago, the first train ride in Germany, from Fuerth to Nuremberg, caused a sensation at a speed of 36 kilometers per hour. At the time, the doors were nailed down for safety to prevent 200 passengers from panicking in the coaches. Today, ICE intercity highspeed trains crisscross countries at approx. 300 km/h, while travelers read a book, or take a nap snuggled up in their cushions. Tomorrow, they will be gliding on rails in rocket-style, high-tech trains, controlled by computers and entirely unaffected by weather conditions.

The power of thought

We need to learn how to tap into future realms and embrace, rather than deny, innovation at last. In doing so, we preserve our energy and add a touch of curiosity to life. Neurophysiologists found that up to 80,000 thoughts cross our minds every day. Yet, we are consciously aware of a mere six percent of all these thoughts. Moreover, such paltry recovery consists of stale, old paradigms, which have a counter-productive effect on one's personal life plan and hamper societal performance. With time, brain activity slackens and our senses are dulled, much like a muscle that is not being exercised. Thanks to methods of modern brain research, we know today that the human brain can form synapses right up into old age, provided that is being exercised. We need to generate stimulation, stretch limits, design visions. Winspiration Day intends to contribute toward such aspirations. Feature film, The Secret, is based on this insight: Through the power of our thoughts, we can become more successful than we could ever have imagined. All we need to do is seize the opportunity and get back to basics – once a year and, indeed, on each and every other day, similar to Valentine's Day, when you take your lover out to dinner and make plans for the future. On May 7, we think ahead! We invite friends and family, neighbors and peers. We meet privately, or in public, and gather momentum, thinking big ... and bigger, yet.

The Purpose:
What life is worth living for

An apple isn't a pear. And no amount of cultivation can change this. The fruit always maintains its own nature at the core. Its appearance and taste can, however, be refined, if conditions are right. It can mature in peace and develop to ripeness. The same is true of the gifts that people carry within. They, too, may not be ignored, so that they can develop into true talents. They must be identified and nurtured. Only then does self-actualization occur. I call this Purpose. It is important to identify this Purpose and to strengthen it in order not to have regrets at the end of one's life and in order to be authentic and happy. A focus day can help – once a year on the 7th of May.

How quickly we suffocate our talents due to deficient education, by choosing the wrong profession for which we toil 60 hours a week and finally collapse with burn-out. I am not impressed by statistics on working hours and proof of performance. Far too often they conceal a personal dilemma.

Statistics are popular in German-speaking countries. In business, especially, every area is examined and described in terms of numbers. As a result they are lent an ostensibly serious note. They describe a treasured truth, which can shake one awake or tempt one to yawn – depending on the topic or perspective.

The Federal Bureau of Statistics indicates: Germans work too much and for overly lengthy periods of time. What do such statistics say about one's personal fate? They calculate the quantity of work, not its quality. In my view the efforts of a nurse in the ICU count more than a teacher's scheduled teaching. Statistics measures professions in terms of figures, not vocations. The joy of working and life's self-fulfillment are ignored. So at the end we have the number of 60 working hours a week that the statisticians remind us of. This leads to debate, in fact, global debate: pessimists wrinkle their foreheads and warn us: "Ethics are in danger. We need a new guideline or we will work ourselves to death." Optimists roll up their sleeves and rejoice: "That's a good sign. It shows that ever more people feel their profession is a vocation, that not time, but a good feeling at the end of the day, is important."

I believe: We do not need working hours with a limit, but an activity that we value and love and of which we know: we are passionate for these tasks. Then overtime hours become superfluous and the 5 p.m. mentality takes care of itself. This topic engrosses Europe and the US. Books on new working structures have become the trend. The old Bismarck retirement age of 65 is finally being dismantled and aligned with demographic changes, the excessive observation of which is unlikely to be constructive in terms of quality of life. Because only the Purpose should be the guide, without an expiration date to limit one's performance. Where would we be in a society with an aging prognosis, if people of 60 + should rust away instead of mixing their life and profession into an elixir of power?

From 65 to 100

For people who find satisfaction for themselves and a purpose for society in their work, the motivation to perform does not stop at

65. This limit is a relic of the century before last, when noise, filth, monotony and wear and tear forced people to age prematurely. Framework conditions at work have changed ages ago. Modern technology and an awareness of such dangers provide health standards nowadays as never before. Working longer is possible. Life-long learning is the magic formula for challenging tasks, for flexibly accompanying the demands of the market and of time. Today no one is still guaranteed a job from their education to their retirement. And this is a good thing. For choice means liberty.

Thanks to hygiene and interdisciplinary research, nutrition and education, people in the Western hemisphere are living longer and longer, so long that the President of Germany was in a position to congratulate 68,104 citizens who were over 100 years old with birthday cards. 100-year-olds are no longer an exception in our society. The elderly are staying fit and alert longer. They want to take part in discussing and shaping the future, to pass on their experiences. What a pool of the spirit of the times and wisdom that subsequent generations can draw from. We need a sensible mix of old and young, of mutual inspiration, in our society. And life-long learning attains a special quality against the backdrop of this development. Empty sayings such as "You can't teach an old dog new tricks" have been scientifically refuted and are not sustainable from a social perspective. Rather, the saying should be: "You can teach an old dog new tricks." Times change, so do insights.

Don't whine – move

The demographic transformation conceals a huge potential of experience. We are on the right path to recognize and exploit this. And I venture to forecast for the future: Europe could succeed in emerging from the financial crisis, which is simply a banking crisis, as a strong region. For the crisis is in my opinion an occasion to reflect on what we need to do to grow together. This is a task and an opportunity at the same time. This will influence the entire planet Earth, even if the population of the old continent will comprise only eight percent.

In order to master this crisis in Europe, three conditions must be fulfilled: the diversity of cultures and languages must be appreciated, democracy must be lived, the entire range of art or entrepreneurial models must be utilized. Think of the major thinkers of the Enlightenment, such as Descartes or Humboldt, of the initial inklings of democracy that emanated from England, of artists such as Dürer, Beethoven, Goethe, Rodin, Picasso, Beuys, of successful family business that combine tradition and innovation, of the endowment culture.

If Europe grows together, if it acts as a reliable partner and always presents its philosophy of freedom as its mission, then a flourishing future is assured. No other part of the earth lives in peace so reliably or has a greater democratic understanding. But this is a fragile commodity. The pressure from the right in Hungary shows this at the moment. In my opinion the 27 countries must coordinate more closely, act jointly and design an idea of the future that includes its citizens, rather than makes them uncertain.

Europe needs programs for education, for health, for happiness and, moreover, for the greatest possible economic freedom, beyond restrictive guidelines and regulations. The brain researcher Professor Manfred Spitzer summarizes this premise: "If we don't change Europe, we will soon be manufacturing T-shirts for China."

Happiness as a basic right

Not only politicians are responsible for the success of the grand project, Europe. Rather, each and every one can contribute to its success. Everyone should ask: What can we do for politics in our country? As John F. Kennedy once encouraged: Don't put your hands in your lap and wait for help from above, rather take your life in your own hands and maybe look past your own garden fence to see how your neighbors are doing. Anyone who lives happily, true to their own capabilities and life views, will render services for themselves and others. Not money, but only personal happiness, should be the engine here. I know men who drive luxury limousines and are worried at the end of the month whether they can pay the rent. When I ask why their car has to be so expensive, they answer: "It's my status symbol." I think the price is too high, though. It restricts action and thus personal freedom. One's head has to remain free for the truly fulfilling tasks, the true opportunities in life.

We all know the great models who reach the very top. Such as Paul McCartney. He has music in his blood and could never imagine doing something else. With or without the Beatles, as soloist or song-writer – everything he took on, he did with passion. Today he is the most successful musician of all time. I am convinced that each individual has an inherent strength, which stubbornly persists in leaving its finger print behind, its traces – even if money is not an issue and abundantly available. Wealth could never prevent a Paul McCartney or a Michael Schumacher from making music or racing cars.

Discovering, developing and living this strength may never be sacrificed to the demands of others. Not in one's profession and, much earlier, not at school. The short fable "The School of Life" talks about this:

> *"Once upon a time, animals had their own school. Lessons consisted of running, climbing, flying and swimming and all animals were taught in all subjects. The duck was good in swimming, even better than the teacher. It was average in flying, but especially hopeless in running. Since it got such bad grades in this subject, it had to stay after school and miss swimming lessons in order to practice running. It did this so long that it was only average in swimming, too. Average grades, however, were acceptable, so no one was concerned about this other than the duck. The eagle was considered a difficult pupil. He beat all others during their climbing lesson, always the first to reach the tip of the tree. But the eagle was harshly and strictly disciplined, since he insisted on using his own method. The rabbit started out being the head of the class in running. But he had a nervous breakdown due to all the additional tutoring hours in swimming and had to leave school [...] At the end of the school year a somewhat unusual eel, who could swim well, run a bit, climb a little bit and even*

fly a little bit, came in first and ended up valedictorian. (Extract from: "The School for Animals" by Georg H. Reavis)

I find nothing more life-threatening than losing a sense of one's own capabilities. On the 2005 Winspiration Day in Berlin, I related an incident that took place in San Francisco:

I sat in a small bar at the harbor in order to relax and watched the fishermen. One of them noticed my rapt observation and spoke to me: "The pelicans almost became extinct." I jumped like someone jolted from a short daydream and looked at the old man questioningly. He raised his arm and guided my glance towards the open ocean: "We barely go out anymore. It's not worth it. This was almost the end for the pelicans. Because they ate the fish intestines that we threw into the sea for them. At some point they forgot how to take care of themselves. They simply couldn't do it anymore. They became thinner and weaker. We were worried. Until one of us had the idea of getting a pelican from far away. One who still knew how things were supposed to work." The old man removed his cap from his head and twisted it between his fingers. He seemed to be searching for words. He looked me straight in the eye. His features softened: "Can you imagine? We got a pelican from the other end of the coast. He actually became an example for ours, who had forgotten how to fish. It was as though this pelican woke what was in the others with a kiss." He cleared his throat and whispered, moved by his story: "Since then we know: everyone in nature has its place. And its capabilities. We cannot suppress this."I laid my hand on his shoulder and answered, deeply moved: "Thank you. Thank you for this wonderful story."

Human dignity

Just as the duck in the fable can swim the best and the eagle fly the highest, people, too, have different inclinations and talents. It is a long-term task for each individual to promote them. Top athletic performance is only possible due to training and fine-tuning special strengths, stamina and envisioning a specific goal. Only an individual program strengthens our physical strength and brightens up the life of society on the whole. Teachers, too, should have this awareness and later professors and, of course, also employers. It should not be bonuses that entice performance. Studies show that the risk of heart attack rises with job dissatisfaction. People experience tasks that do not fit them as a top stress factor. Over the years they destroy themselves. The fashionable term, work-life balance, does not change this.

| http://may7.org/hpnv – The Nonsense of "Work-Life Balance" (German)

There is no compensation for the suffocating feeling of accomplishing tasks that are not in line with one's own destination. Nevertheless, companies believe they can keep their employees in a good mood with appealing mottos. They formulate guidelines such as: "We assure a work-life balance for our employees." "We appreciate each of our employees." "We train and foster our employees. But such sentences don't have any impact if they are only written down. Only actions bring success; companies must observe very closely what makes their employees tick. Each individual should be able to formulate his or her personal expectation of his or her profession and deploy his or her talents correspondingly. We don't need equality; we need different talents for a variety of tasks. We need our view of life, our Purpose, in order to create a vocation from a profession, in order to create a life's work from our daily routine.

But how do people discover their Purpose? The seed is planted in childhood. From there it can grow and blossom. And, with a great deal of luck, a child will experience loving supervision and basic trust and the words of parents and teachers: "You are fine as you are. But never tire of making the effort of doing your best. Learn with discipline; reach your goals. I will help you if you wish. I think that this is the interpretation of Article 1 of the basic right "Human dignity is inalienable". To live up to one's own potential, not to tire, to get the best from oneself – this is protection against suffering, depression and burnout. It is the method of choice to protect oneself against lack of autonomy. Everyone should know, however, where his or her own personal limit is, so as not to get lost and to afford protection from artificial goals.

Rhyming like Ringelnatz

During puberty, children want to set their boundaries, want to learn who they are and what they want. School, however, wants conformity – with respect to the class, the rules and, especially, the study plans.

At age 14 I thought it was ridiculous to recite the rhymes of Ringelnatz, the clapping rhythm of which took precedence over the content. I thought it was superfluous to stand in front of the class quoting Christian Morgenstern. How should I know what he thought about the seagull Emma while composing the poem? I didn't want to interpret it. I didn't see the sense in it. He admitted himself that he only wrote this nonsense for the rhyme. His weasel poem says: "A weasel sat on chisel in a stream's drizzle. Do you know why? The calf in the moon told me at a quiet time: the refined animal did it for the rhyme." So there...

I wanted company, stimulation, ideas for discovering my ego. So I was considered a grumber, a trouble-maker. I withdrew. I remember standing at the foot of the stairs to the school.

> The bell rang. And before I could go up the steps – never skipping a step, since I was in no hurry to get to class – hundreds of pupils came towards me, running, talking, laughing or in silence. They came towards me and the individual disappeared in the crowd. They all ran down the stairs at the same rhythm. I thought: if one of them were missing, it wouldn't be noticed. This made me sad and at the same time I realized: I don't want to walk in step. I want something else, something out of the ordinary that belongs only to me, that makes sense to me.

Now I know, I was looking for my own thing, for my Purpose. Teachers, however, don't see this, even now.

It would be decades before I would find my destination as a mentor. As so many young people, I had no clear idea where my journey was headed. There were detours, for I did not have the courage to discover my paths all by myself. So I tromped down broad roads.

I did what my parents liked, what friends chose. Initially I studied electrical engineering. More on this topic later.

Young people at the threshold of the professional world usually lack orientation. How great it is to know at age 18, 19, 20, where the professional journey will take you. I became an attorney and entrepreneur. I grew wealthy, flew throughout Europe in private jets. I did not find happiness in these flights. On the contrary. My soul was sick and sad, I slid into depression because of the small spark of long ago, when I refused to recite the rhymes of Morgenstern, when I didn't want to drown in the pablum of school education, this small spark never stopped smoldering. But at the same time this was lucky for me. In my sadness I realized: whining doesn't help. Whining means standing still and, in a worst-case scenario, unconsciousness. I needed to get moving to achieve my three major life goals, which are no different from the seven billion people on this earth: to be healthy, happy and financially independent.

I realized: for a long time I had directed my attention only to the last wish – I equated my happiness with monetary wealth. The two other coordinates, health and happiness, had disappeared and my view of life had been drained of color. Since then I have become convinced that the human drive for self-preservation is of such enormous strength that anyone can pull themselves out of a crisis. This feeling saved me. At some point I had a brainstorm that suddenly changed my interior world: often adults visit the places of their youth when depressed. They want to remember the strength of their younger years, they want to feel like people whose future is at their feet. I did this, too. I drove to Berlin at the lowest point of my identity crisis.

Where would my thoughts rest? Where would I be able to rea-waken my joy in the future? While I strolled the streets of Berlin, wondering at the haste of the pedestrians and their inconsiderate pace, I was drawn to the University, to the cafeteria. The loud clanging of dishes, the chairs sliding, the laughter and talk of students rushed towards me, absorbed me in this room of concrete and steel. It looked, sounded and smelled the same as always. Time appeared to have stood still. Students ate breakfast, talking with their mouths full. I sat down with them and became a listener right away. "That's the end! I'm quitting. The sentence sounded very decisive and led to a vehement discussion at the next table. "Are you crazy?" "So close to your goal? In a year you will have passed the state examination!" The fellow students opened their eyes wide. "What do you even plan to do?" "I've thought about this a lot. I don't want to be a lawyer. I don't want to start a fight and I don't want to settle one either. I don't want to get into a fighting arena and fix what others have messed up. That's not how I want to earn money." "That's occurred to your rather early! So what do you want?" "To stay at home and be there for our baby. Silent bewilderment. And during this break the young man who was in the midst of ending his career, before it could start, provided his statement: "My wife and I decided together: I will be the house-husband and have her back. She will work in crisis zones as a reporter." Somewhat impolitely, but having become curious, I turned around, looked the future university dropout and house-husband in the eye and congratulated him spontaneously on his clarity and courage. And this gesture was in part for me. For – I and I alone can give my life sense. Not doctors, not psychologists, not discussion partners and not friends. Only on his own can one discover what is essential in life.

The little spark from the past ignited once again. It could no longer be ignored — I wanted to live my special capability, my strength. I wanted to work with people, support them in discovering their capabilities. As mentor, as speaker. I was finally able to put in a nutshell what I was hearing within: Drop the job. End the career that brings you money, a great deal of money, that allows you to have a private jet, a yacht and a life of luxury. Be radical at the height of your success and throw everything that makes you heavy or sad overboard. I did it. And even if someone had told me that I would live off unemployment insurance for the rest of my days, it wouldn't have stopped me. For too long I had fought as an attorney for clients, for too long I had forgotten my own Purpose. And with this decision ideas were ignited in me that felt good. I smiled for the first time in a long time. Not just with the corners of my mouth, but with all my heart. This felt right. Perhaps the others, the pedestrians in Berlin, saw this too. They didn't seem as hectic to me; rather, they looked into my eyes and at times we nodded at one another in passing. I saw children who ran after their mothers and believed that everything would be all right.

I wanted to work with people, to give them an idea for their lives, beyond Ringelnatz in school and beyond their parental home, those who lived off social security, later to become Hartz IV (welfare benefits for long-term unemployed), still remaining only a euphemism for poverty.

So I chose my other path. The decision was under the motto — there is life before death. The bestseller by Bronnie Ware: "5 things that the dying regret" shows how relevant this insight is today.

The author has touched a nerve with her book. The fear of wasting one's one life seems ubiquitous. At the end of their days, people who have not lived according to their destination regret each lost second: "I would have been happy to have the courage to live my own life and not be guided by the expectations of others." Or: "I should have granted myself more happiness and satisfaction."

This remorse can be avoided provided we think of the purpose of our lives on a daily basis. Plus once a year. If we combine our strength with others, we raise our energy by multiples. A vision of happiness can be created on this day of the year, the 7th of May. People close to each other on large stages with impressive programs, as well as in small spaces at home, have a common dream: that of a fulfilled future. This dream comes true with the belief that "The Best is Yet to Come."

The Human Development Index –
A four-note chord of education,
health, happiness and money

People in Bangladesh are suffering – from natural disasters and the depletion of forests in the Himalayas. The trees that once regulated the water masses of the Ganges, Meghna and Brahmaputra rivers are no longer alive. Wealthy countries need wood. They burn it and process it. Since then the delta around Dhaka has flooded. Harvests are destroyed and sometimes houses and all worldly possessions.

The country is suffering from climate change. The Northern part of the world is blithely propelling it forward in a race for the best gross national product. But Bangladesh cannot sprint. Poverty is a paralyzing force. Nutrition and hygiene are lacking. Children toil rather than attend school. The future of girls appears similar to the role of their mothers. They have to obey. And if they dream of something other than the reality of work and obedience, this would have consequences. There are reports of hydrochloric acid attacks by rejected husbands and of so-called honor killings ever since fundamentalists have instigated these acts among the population. This is intimidating. Men and women who have never learned to defend themselves against despotism do not trust in change. They lack education and courage. Illiteracy rates in rural areas are almost 90 percent. Infant mortality is 97 for every thousand births. It was 1990, when the United Nations published its "Human Development Report" for the first time. An economist from South Asia developed the criteria – one who knew the conditions and who knew: a country only achieves change, if it contributes to the happiness of its citizens. Mahbub ul Haq directed his research towards human development and his focus at South Asia around Bangladesh.

Vision

Ul Haq had a goal: He wanted to be able to compare development among countries. He doubted that the sum of all products and services would be the right basis. He did not find the statistics moral, because these annual results combined statements of poor quality with tales of disease, catastrophes and strokes of fate. Together with his friend Amartya Sen of India and additional colleagues he designed a formula to measure human happiness. This formula is complicated, contains values that determine congruencies. For an action follows each intention and each action has a consequence for itself and others. This formula consists of coordinates, threshold values and lines on which indices are multiplied, divided and merged with one another again. This is the theory, the mathematical equation of happiness, that one can find in the UN "Human Development Report". It is composed of the values of education, health, nutrition, hygiene and life expectancy.

Development opportunities

In 2013 the report appears for the 23rd time. (http://may7.org/mspb.) It focuses a burning lens on the duties of the government in promoting development, enabling education, guaranteeing trade and innovation and safeguarding rights. And it also guides the focus to citizens who wish to determine their own lives. Based on these reports we can tell that people are happier the more they are part of the discussion, determination and the mix overall. We learn how calming an effect social welfare has on personal crises such as unemployment and disability. Short-term support spurs people to get up after crises, roll up their sleeves and start on something new. People want equality of opportunity. India recognized this when it decreed by law that 25 percent of the desirable spots in each private school in the country be assigned to children from vulnerable circumstances. And Bangladesh recognized this with its programs to strengthen the role of women in society. Today the figures in the tables, the columns in the graphs show a completely different result than in 1990: The infant mortality rate is decreasing. The illiteracy rate is down. Women work in craft and industry. They are organizing themselves, led by non-governmental organizations, in groups, educating themselves in health, nutrition and hygiene. They even venture to take the step into independence, supported by Muhammad Yunus and his micro-credit program through the Grameen Bank.

The emerging countries of Brazil and India are undergoing similar developments. Together with China they will constitute approximately 40 percent of global production by 2050, according to the report.

You don't have to be clairvoyant to know that facts will continue to change. While England was once a world power, the former leader in industrialization is now quiet. Rolls Royce and Jaguar are now owned by Indian families. iPhones and iPads started their success story in the US and are now being produced in China to a major extent. This fact shows: We are living together on earth. The Brazilian author, Paulo Coelho, is one of the most popular authors of the present and his words are not only literary, but also political. They substantiate the claim of the Human Development Index: "Ultimately it is about sharing. And this is part of human nature in my view. We don't just give money: our goal is independence – and we get a lot back for that."

█ http://may7.org/ndle – Interview with Yunus/Coelho (German)

Relationships

The South and the North are moving closer together – this harbors wonderful opportunities: The Best is yet to come, once people understand that not profit alone should be in the forefront, but a 4-note chord of education and health, happiness and money. ul Haq speaks intelligently on this: "People unite around the world in a common effort: They want to participate actively and freely in events and activities that shape their lives."

This assumes that politicians will draw the framework for people's participation wide and generously and that the people on their part are ready to take over responsibility for themselves. For themselves and their families. It's not about putting your hands in your lap. I think that a mayor who hops from one party to the next, who comments on wasting billions in the new construction of the new Berlin Airport by shrugging his shoulders and, when difficulties arise, trades his Supervisory Board post with his then vice-mayor, is not taking his job seriously. Political responsibility is not about sleight of hand, but honest confessions in clear words, such as: "That was a mistake. I apologize."

The affluent North in Europe is worried. Rather than uncertainty at all levels, rather than Euro doubts, we need the courage to persist and programs that place people's talents at their very core. Otherwise the risk arises that a downward spiral is created, led by fear: Then companies dismiss their employees. Then families dispense with consumption, education and sports. Then food is purchased because it is cheap and health gradually evaporates. The North, rich and generous, is showing small surface scratches. The formula for happiness can also be a seismograph for small downwards changes.

Responsibility

Let us then reflect on our power to persist, to find creative solutions. Let us exploit opportunities to continue our upward trend. I think it is fascinating how developments change once thoughts of catastrophe are no longer the focus, but rather a belief in qualitative growth and qualitative wealth. This, too, is the idea of the Winspiration Days. Positive thoughts about the future have a greater effect than doom-mongering. There are always two perspectives for any goal. And I clearly prefer the positive one, the view of happiness. Life consists of change. Anything else means standing still. With a responsible attitude towards the changes that time brings, we can solve problems, create modern and free forms of work, refrain from an overly critical view of innovation and new technologies. An African proverb says: "If different music is playing, a new dance comes, too."

Higher level

I call the focus on what really counts „Purpose living". An awareness of special talents should start early, in one's childhood years. A two-year-old feels his ego for the first time and has a sense of his own charisma. Parents who recognize this and strengthen it with a gentle hand are undertaking a wonderful thing. They are encouraging their child to feel joy. They laugh together. And – they allow sadness, not simply wiping it away with comforting words. Consolation is well-intentioned, but, if expressed too early, fails to take children's moods seriously. Good parents show: We see that you are sad and are with you. So the child can choose how intensively and how long his sadness should continue. He is always aware that he is right the way he is and the way he feels.

A child can discover himself with this self-image. He can learn to take his intentions seriously from when he is very young. He can expect praise rather than contempt for his actions. He grows strong in social and empathetic skills. Children who are parented in such an intelligent manner have no need to run riot at school as young people. And they will not end up on social welfare as adults. They will always maintain a belief in themselves in life, even in difficult situations. People are not born to be taken care of by the government or by companies. They are born to contribute their reason, to design their visions. They want to be part of a group, recognize values and contribute to society together with others in a moral understanding. People are the true wealth of this world.

And their claim to happiness is a universal one, even though it may be fulfilled in very different ways – sleeping on a bare floor is enough for a monk; an aid worker is moved by a grateful embrace; an entrepreneur takes pride in the distinction of being the best employer among medium-sized companies. No matter what an individual's goals are, they represent a striving towards happiness. Rank and title and a shy glance to ascertain the appreciation of others are no longer important with this outlook; the accumulation of money is experienced as a stress factor to be overcome. There is no question that money can create joy and can cushion the struggle for survival. But as soon as money becomes a purpose in and of itself, things go awry. So for me one sentence remains at the end as the essence of all thoughts on happiness: It is not about a decision between happiness or affluence, purpose or profit. It is about multiplying both at a higher level.

Values

How can one measure happiness? Researchers into happiness say that it is not the chase for profits or the efforts for efficiency that are key, but rather knowledge of one's own strength, of the possibility of changing things and positively shaping the general good. It can be measured based on one's own satisfaction and that of others. The Kingdom of Bhutan recognized this when it announced approximately thirty years ago that it would prepare a report on gross national happiness every year. Employees of the royal super ministry survey the kingdom's population annually. A glance at the results, always tinged with Buddhist philosophy, could provide a prediction for a few politicians and entrepreneurs in the rich countries of this earth. Perhaps the Schlecker family would have understood earlier that an empire cannot be built on greed. A company can only be successful over the long term if it nurtures a culture of appreciation and promotes its employees. Anything else is false and destined for failure. Maybe managers would have learned earlier that profiting oneself does not bring profit over the long term and avoided the legal restrictions on salaries. And perhaps the sad discussion on a quota of women would have become obsolete, since performance and dedication cannot be reduced to a number.

Faith

Yes, I believe happiness can be measured. This is why we have designed a happiness form in the Winspiration Day Association and ask our members to fill it out. We analyze the responses and give every member feedback. The criteria of the Human Development Index are the basis for the happiness form. We would like to add another facet to this: one's own spirituality. This grows in us from the time of our birth. It can be a strength in adverse conditions and even keep us from losing our courage to live after strokes of fate. Aung San Suu Kyi, Burma's freedom fighter, spent more than twenty years under house arrest dictated by the military junta. She did not allow her will to be broken and kept her faith in a good future: "Let us join hands to create a peaceful world, one in which we can sleep in safety and awaken full of joy." There are visions that never lose their luster.

Opportunities –
Crises are challenges

As a monk he teaches modesty. As a spiritual leader, he spreads the word of compassion. He does not tire speaking about his Middle-Way Approach, which is to end in Tibet's religious, cultural and linguistic freedom.

Tibetans have been living under the control of China since 1951. And no voice among the international community has been able to change that until today. The Dalai Lama lives in exile. He gives his people courage with his faith in a return to Lhasa. He was honored with the Nobel Peace Prize in 1989 for his philosophy of non-violent dialogue. Since this act of respect the modest man has become an example for many who find themselves in hopeless situations.

When the Dalai Lama talks about the clarity of thought in lectures, about living in the here and now, then tens of thousands of people undertake the pilgrimage to listen to him, to think in silence. They hope to discover the purpose of life in these hours together. "Take happiness in the small things of life, the large things will come by themselves", he advises his listeners. Confidence and a healthy dose of patience, even surrender, can be heard through his message and whoever keeps this sentence as a mantra will guide his thoughts into a more positive direction. Because he is focused on the present, on the many small successes of each and every day. On happiness at the other end of effort. From Greenland to the Tierra del Fuego, all around the world people want to discover the secret to happiness; perhaps it will be unveiled by the pure, unadulterated insight that people live in order to be happy.

Forgotten happiness

The first prerequisite for happiness is the end of suffering – this is a Buddhist saying. If it were only so simple. For many, suffering begins anew every day. They make their way to a job that they barely appreciate and this is precisely the crux of the matter: they don't like their tasks. They say to themselves: The money is not enough and there are no alternatives. They are, however, tapping right into this economic profit system – they don't want to, but there is nothing else on offer. Or is there?

> *When I debated many years ago as a young man with my German high school certificate in my pocket how I would earn my daily bread to start with, I asked my parents for advice and looked over my classmates" shoulders to see what they were doing as far as education and studies were concerned. Two of them decided to study electrical engineering and took up a three-month internship at Siemens. This was mandatory before starting one's studies. Everyone nodded to me: "Engineer, son, become an engineer; they are always needed."*

> *For lack of arguments and alternatives I applied with Siemens and started practical training. Nowadays it would be called a trainee program. It would be perfectly organized and peppered with learning goals, but in those days the path to being a production engineer led straight to the workshop. Theory gave way to practice. I worked at the conveyor belt from –the first days, starting punctually at 6:30 a.m. My card was stamped every morning and every evening. In the meantime I*

screwed together railway signals. I felt lonely in this monotony. The men were not happy to be here – that was my impression. They tried to shorten the hours, find some pastimes in order to outwit the attendance clock, by showering in the changing rooms rather than at home. This counted towards their working hours and saved leisure time. The restrained conduct on the part of my colleagues increasingly astonished me. It was only when a younger student trainee revealed to me: "They are always like that here. This is normal. They are afraid that you will become their supervisor after your training," I took note. Was this what professional life looked like? Tricking the attendance clock and interacting poorly with colleagues? I looked around and saw their tired faces. They were stuck in a job that would never fulfill them. What a waste of life! The man who entered the workshop in the morning first, who operated the machines by pushing a button and thus drew a framework around the work was the technical engineer by the way. I finished my three-month internship and not a day more. But I never forgot the experience of how work can have a dulling influence.

Making money does not mean forgetting about life. On the contrary, if one's profession becomes a vocation, then people blossom. I find the equation worded „To work means to find happiness" much more appealing. I am happy to follow the United Nations in this position. They are endeavoring to measure the happiness factor in countries in addition to profits. As no other instrument does, the Human Development Index shows that countries are more satisfied the higher their health, education and freedom for individual life styles. And this intention almost sounds spiritual. In line with the words of the Dalai Lama to enjoy the moment, each of the 28,800 seconds of an average working day should be seen as a transitory treasure. But this perspective of happiness is always forgotten when greed is the guiding factor. And money is never the Purpose.

Hospitals, the economic system of which consists in increasing subsidies by means of the volume of operations, lead the appreciation of the human individual ad absurdum. If medical students were to address their substantive focus towards maintaining health, rather than towards illness, as early as at the university stage, then the whole moral concept would be different. The scalpel would not then be used to compensate for administrative and financial deficits, but only to save lives. Operations would not become sources of funds. Advice, prevention and selecting options for maintaining and ensuring health over the long term would be the ethical focus. There is no examination subject called Health in the university education system. A 180 degree rotation in approach is required. The goal in a hospital with a high ethical mission statement should be to make operations superfluous.

Opportunities grow through self-initiative

I would like to clarify this thought with a response from the Nobel Peace Prize recipient Muhammad Yunus.

Between 350,000 and 500,000 small children become blind in developing countries every year. The German emergency doctors of Cap Anamur raise the alarm. Bangladesh, too, laments this great suffering. Muhammad Yunus visits many families in rural areas. He had already recognized the link between this childhood disease and the poverty of the families early on. He developed his program of aid for self-aid. He founded a micro-credit institute in order to distribute small amounts without delay directly to people who come to him with an entrepreneurial idea, wanting thus to escape poverty. Yunus offers them an opportunity that might mean only the cost of 27 dollars for a set of pots. For instance, he saved a man struggling for survival in so doing. From then on the recipient of the micro-credit has been cooking dishes and selling them from the side of the road.

Poor people should be able to build up a feeling of self-worth and rediscover their pride, lost as the result of begging, by working and earning their own money. Yunus has found many imitators and international recognition since with his Grameen Bank. Newspapers are full of praise for this type of development aid and the Nobel Peace Prize raised the professor of economics into the circle of globally valued experts. Yunus used these contacts when the rate of blindness rose. He sought information world-wide from experts in order to learn more about the reasons for this eye disease in his home country. Only a few letters and discussions were needed to initiate a research project with large pharmaceutical companies. They soon found out together – the reason is a vitamin A deficiency. Nutrition from rice contains too much carbohydrate and not enough protein and vitamins. The cornea softens and clouds over. Small children thus lose their vision. Furthermore, the conjunctiva dry out, weakening the immune system. For children who go blind due to such nutritional errors, there is no cure. They will never be able to see again; no operation can correct this. Often these children die before reaching school age.

Each member of the team was deeply concerned and wanted to help quickly and in straightforward fashion, offering to provide the children with vitamin A pills. This was supposed to take place without any bureaucracy, in fact without licenses. One could start a multi-year project was the common consensus. Yunus refused. To the astonishment of all, he said: "I don't want this kind of help." "Why not? You are well known in Bangladesh. Mothers trust you. With your help we will be able to reach the poorest families in rural areas and be allowed to treat their children." Yunus shook his head. "But we can get these families to take the pills every day. Why don't you want to accept such uncomplicated help? It will protect against further blindness," the Western researchers objected. The Asian stubbornness of the Professor was incomprehensible. But Yunus was not stubborn. He was worried. He looked farther into the country's future, thought of the dependency that would arise from this project. "This, ladies and gentlemen, cannot be the right solution. It is often better to not take only one step, but rather to take many additional steps in spirit and reflect on the consequences. We don't want charity. We want nutrition in our country." Sources of vitamin A include carrots, peppers and mangoes. Muhammad Yunus suggested cultivating all the fruit and vegetable types that form carotenoids in the villages. It would create jobs and give people the sensible tasks of sowing and harvesting, selling and commercializing. It would teach the families how nutrition works, how food chains arise and keep the body healthy. "Only then can true assistance exist, since people understand the value of their work, because they see a deep satisfaction in maintaining health. Only when we change our doctrines and question our behavior, adapting them to the times again and again, can we make opportunities from crises." Since then the economics professor has granted many micro-credits in the agricultural sector and has a story or two to tell. And Yunus achieved even more. The children's blindness is known throughout the world. Readiness to help grows constantly. New concepts are introduced and tested. Why? Because the farmers are not holding out their hands, but working. Confidence that they can promise their children a better future is steadily building.

Using one's own initiative is contagious. It is more beneficial than help imposed from one institution to another, by one government on another. Too easily dependencies can develop when the needs of the individual is not sufficiently considered. No matter how NGOs try to focus on the human being and his welfare, there is still a risk that projects will fail because donations are inadequate or that projects are approved only because they promise media resonance or sharpen a particular image. This feeling creeps up on me when institutions advertise their activities as helpers in the third world. There can"t be a third world in my opinion: Which was the first, which was the second world? There is no such thing. We live together on this wonderful planet Earth and have the responsibility of protecting it and handing it over intact to our children and grandchildren. I wish that every human being would discover what power is in inside him, what he can do for himself and the common good.

True opportunities only become apparent in a crisis. Those who have been at the very bottom know: A small spark of hope can still be felt even in dark days. I have often experienced how fast one can go up again provided one identifies strength under one's own initiative or with the initial help of others. There are examples of such fates and they always touch us deeply. They give us courage, throw out an anchor in difficult times. I learned this especially in my Kids Coaching: sometimes only a small ignition is necessary in order to be able to see the future clearly and brightly. As soon as the courage to live is awakened again, as soon as responsibility for one's own effectiveness results in performance, success stories are created. It is immaterial where in the world this small jolt to the ego takes place; people recognize their opportunities. This applies to all continents; I experienced this in Europe, America, Asia and also in Africa.

A song in Africa

Twice I got involved in "Kids Coaching". In 2005 I did so together with Bob Proctor. It was my wish to work with, talk to and provide topics not included in curricula in meetings and telephone calls with children and young people. What do you enjoy? What are you good at? How can you support others? I want to coach them far from school stress in order to give them an idea of their own life design, in order to discover their individual capabilities together with them. The quintessence of these years is: Children are happy to learn, easily enthused, performance-oriented. They don't need grades for this. They learn of their own free will. Because It's fun and because they recognize the potential inside them. Looking back I can say that social levels do not play a role and do not impair learning, if children are fostered according to their talents. They develop strengths and ideas and cannot be held back from their fantasies of the future. And this is the case all over the world.

As part of an NGO project, the co-writer of this book, Gabriele Borgmann, traveled to Senegal. She was to shoot a film with a camera team about neglected children who were offered a school education as part of this project. These children lived close to Dhaka. They can be found quickly by car. The slums begin where the asphalted road stops, where a path with potholes narrows, the houses become shacks, the windows become holes and are covered in rags. Small children sit in red dust and a steamy cloud of alcohol permeates the heat. The fathers are drinkers. They steal and sell the goods in illegal markets near the slums. The mothers are prostitutes and collapse in later years. You don't need a lot of imagination to figure out where these children will end up some day.

In the middle of this misery a school project was started up. In part against the will of the parents, employees of a European institution dressed the children in school uniforms. The picked up the small ones for their lessons every morning and brought them home again every evening clean, well-nourished and with eyes shining. The children soon started to love this rickety school. It was surrounded by a wooden fence and had holes in the roof. It was their refuge. A small fountain was the meeting point in the schoolyard, old baobob trees provided shade.

Inside sat 50 small alert children in rows and stared at the blackboard with fascination. The team members were allowed to be guests in this elementary school near the slums of Dhaka for one day. They looked into the curious eyes of the children, stroked their wiry hair. They sat down with them, wondering at the tidiness of the tables and the care they took with their notebooks. At the end of the day the children said goodbye with a song. The little tykes, five and six years of age, sang "All my ducks" in a mix of French and English. They laug-

hed heartily and boisterously – the world moved together a little more. The odd tear was gulped down.

Children want to learn and perform extraordinary things. They are looking for their opportunities in life. It is the task of adults to do everything to ensure that they broaden their vision to this end. Children who are able to experience this develop resilience in life. They can adapt to the most varied situations later as adults, but they will never give up their own Purpose. They will always have the courage and the strength to reflect on what they can really do. They will contribute to the Human Development Index measuring the true coordinates for happiness: health, education, freedom in designing one's life.

The Freedom –
Designing one's own life

Freedom is a huge concept. Freedom in the context of the Winspiration Day Association means that everyone may develop according to their capabilities and talents, that they take on responsibility for themselves and for others. Freedom also means that misuse of power and compulsion are not permitted, that, according to Emmanuel Kant, the freedom of the individual stops where the freedom of the next person is restricted. And in between everyone should realize their individual life plans, discover their Purpose from the time of childhood. With respect to the Winspiration Day Association, freedom grows daily with ideas and the courage to shine beyond mediocrity.

Even though I know that much has to improve, I still want to point out: The political and economic situation in the Western world offers fertile ground. We are not ruled by dictators. We can look to tomorrow without fear of despotism. Democracy and the rule of law guarantee this. Our system of a free market economy rewards performance and promotes affluence. This ground of peace and freedom extends before us for the first time in history. This has not always been the case. We don't have to look far back in order to appreciate the value of freedom, in order to nurture it as a valuable commodity, to surround it with our full attention so that it never dies. We have only been enjoying freedom under the law for approximately 60 years. This time interval is like the blink of an eye in history and is only now arriving in our daily routine, in companies, schools and families.

The Winspiration Day Association would like to provide stimuli once a year and to spread inspiration. It would like to offer a stage for freedom for self-realization. Once a year, on May 7th, it would like to focus thought on the enormous responsibility each individual bears for his or her own future and that of the children. On this day and beyond, it would like to encourage people to discover their own strengths and to believe: The Best is yet to come. How would it be to pause and reflect on the Purpose, on what really counts, for once? We know from quantum physics the intensity with which synergy works. How probabilities turn to good, purely due to the will of the observer. We know that developments take a positive turn, if we accompany them with good energy. There are innumerable examples of a whole classroom full of neglected and violence-prone children rising to a high-performance class due to the teacher's committed attitude.

If teachers believe in their pupils without pause and restriction, children will give their best. And then they will learn to keep their composure in life.

Happiness and money

Today we can ask what we want and can develop what we can do. I will go one step further and say: each of us has a duty to emit sparks for ourselves and society as a whole based on our talents. "Where there are gifts, there are duties" – that's the formula for happiness.

Happiness is woven from light material. Not from the thought of money. We don't eat, after all, in order to increase the blood flow through our body. Rather, we eat and drink, ideally the right things, in order to remain healthy and continue to participate in life with all our senses. It is similar in the case of working and earning money: whoever is active only in order to accumulate money is betraying his soul. Happiness and satisfaction fall by the wayside at some point. Companies who see their purpose only as raising the number of invoices issued, rather than paying attention to the quality of the performance and the point of commerce, have no future in the market. They bleed to death. Pero Mićić, futurologist and speaker at the Winspiration Day 2006 in Baden-Baden, writes in this respect: "We must design our companies in such a way that they are not sales growth junkies. We must be free of the addiction to and dependency on growth. [...]. If there should be persistent growth anywhere, it should be in quality of life, regardless of level. Of course with the proviso that we will not treat our planet in such a short-sighted and reckless manner any more."

Bankers who lose billions in order to generate personal profit cause an overall economic collapse, a crisis. It is high time to handle our freedom responsibly, under our own responsibility, and reflect on the consequences of our actions. Whoever really strengthens his strengths and plans his career according to individual criteria and morals, will achieve top performance and financial security. Then we no longer need strikes. Unions can finally change their language and issue a call to working for a purpose rather than the struggle to work. Perhaps they will even become completely superfluous. Nobody should allow themselves to be lured with promises of minimum wages, let themselves be restricted in their capabilities, be paid less than what they are worth. This would ultimately end in human catastrophe. It is much more promising to plan and develop one's capabilities in grand style. Once unions have managed the transformation to structural change in which life-long learning can find a place, in which hierarchical steps are flat and people have a feeling of self-worth, then unions have arrived at their peak. Then train drivers who lay down their duties for one Euro fifty more in wages an hour and cause losses in the millions in this country will no longer be applauded. Everyone is free to leave their job if the conditions no longer suit.

New technologies, different working hour models, greater room for maneuver for individuals will impact the future and go beyond the eight-hour day punctuated by the attendance clock and salary increases calculated up to one's retirement. The best is yet to come, provided people open their eyes and become brave. Pericles already knew this: "The secret of freedom is courage".

Courage to achieve your goal

When I created Winspiration Day in 2003, I wanted to tell stories of people who live for their freedom, who don't let anything stop them, regardless of the fate they may have suffered. In the words of Marianne Williamson: "There is nothing enlightened about shrinking so that other people won't feel insecure around you. And as we let our own light shine, we unconsciously give other people permission to do the same. As we are liberated from our own fear, our presence automatically liberates others. "

The words still echo today and could be the credo for all young people to hold on to their dreams of life, to never give up, even under adverse conditions.

Difficulties for young people already start at school. Films such as "Coach Carter" tell the story. I became aware of this when I coached young people, together with Bob Proctor, in order to give them an idea of the future. The parents supported our project of motivating their children without grade stress and performance pressure. And what happened was so much more than working for good class work in a standard system. The young people lost their fear of learning. The discussions, listening, watching and discovering alone spurred them on to be better. "I have now realized that no-one in my class has goals. Not even the teacher," a fourteen-year-old boy explained to me. What treasures lie there sleeping and are covered up on a daily basis by the lack of imagination of our school curricula. When these young people stood on the stage on Winspiration Day 2006 and announced, upright and with refreshing openness, into the microphone: "It feels so good to know what I can do". "My grades are getting better. Not because I am learning more, but because others accept me." "I am standing here and simply say what I think. This is just great. Thanks!"- the parents were touched and had tears in their eyes. Working with young people and hearing about their ideas on life at some point, those are wonderful moments. And I hope that they can hold on to their idea all their lives, much like Nelson Mandela held on to his life's plan. We need such terrific examples.

One trigger for Winspiration Day was the comment of Federal Chancellor Angela Merkel in 2003 that two million children lived from social security in Germany, one of the wealthiest countries in the world. Children from poor families have more difficulties in kindergarten, schools and their jobs than children of rich families. Their parents have often given up on ife. Communication barely takes place at home. Their vocabulary deteriorates. The creation of synapses in the brain cannot occur. Statistics show that children in conditions of poverty are average linguistically prior to the school holidays and dramatically below average at the end of holidays. Poor children escape into digital worlds more often than others and the downwards spiral is faster. Such children lack inspiration. Dr. Manfred Spitzer showed in his book on "Digital Dementia – How we are causing ourselves and our children to lose our minds" how speech and learning disorders arise. Manfred Spitzer received the Winspiration Day Award in 2010 for his research on brain-appropriate learning and a joyful life.

▌ http://may7.org/emhi – Presentation by Prof. Dr. Spitzer (German)

Poor children do not learn how to fulfill themselves. Not at home and not elsewhere. Their space is narrow, limited by their circumstances. And according to my experience I know – we must change our educational content. And must do everything to lift these children out of the dilemma of poverty. Children need examples to show them that it is worth fighting for your own way. Joana Zimmer never stopped believing in her talent and diligently going her way. The young singer appears on international stages successfully nowadays. She is blind and never quarreled with her fate. Maren Opfermann put sports in the center of her young life. She believed in her breakthrough. She became world champion in wheel gymnastics and now coaches young people herself on the way to their goal.

It is wrong to show pupils in secondary schools how to fill out welfare applications. Rather, we need a new, free subject in the curriculum to show young people how to conscientiously handle their responsibility and strengthen their individual capabilities.

Freedom as a school subject

Our education system focuses on collectivism. Not on individual capabilities. Framework plans are viewed in the light of specifications, compromises and tradition. Each region mixes up its pablum, spicing it up according to taste. Young people are supposed to consume this. Without question. Mandatory schooling is packaged in a vacuum without an expiry date. It has been the same for approximately 200 years; but nothing changes more quickly than time. Multi-layered solutions have been needed for a long time now. A look at the US or France shows a vague trend: home schooling. There are success stories about children who have never attended school and received their education outside the classroom – at home, at relatives' homes, in small private educational groups. But they were still successful at work and in life. How big a step it would be in Germany if parents were put into a position of dealing responsibly with the subject "Freedom" and to pay attention more to life goals than to learning goals.

Or why don't we look at India – private universities have an elite status. Here the students graduate in record time, because they choose their modules themselves. Because the joy of research is in the forefront, not a sprint through a predetermined course of study.

The freer young people feel, the more the sense of the future will grow. We can fall on the way to our goal. We can experience failure. But we should not be satisfied with the mediocre or set ourselves up to be poor.

Into the future with consistency

I know the heights and also the fall: I was very successful many years ago. My attorney's practice and tax consultation business flourished, my real estate company took on huge projects. The façade shimmered on the outside. At the time I thought I had to continue on and on down this career path and became alienated from myself in this speed rush. This had consequences – I got entangled in my work. Running the rat race made me breathless. I lost the feeling for personal freedom. And at the end I stood there with a mountain of debt of approximately 2.5 million Deutschmarks. The downfall hit me hard.

At this nadir, I swore to myself: If the path upwards ever opened up again for me, then I would take it in self-determination and individualism. And I recognized my opportunities with this free vision. A change in perspective took place.

Since then I know – when paradigms shift the petty dance around the golden calf comes to a halt. Then earning money is not the purpose in life, but the effect that occurs when performance grows and promotes joy.

A change in perspective frees us from negative suggestions and allows us to formulate wishes again. We need creativity rather than competition. We need win-win, not lose-lose. So that growth can take place beyond restrictions. Steve Jobs started by tinkering in a garage. He was laughed at. He was driven by his vision.

And he never stopped burning for this vision. 20 years later, Apple is the most expensive company in the world and has revolutionized a number of areas of business. Jobs took the liberty of starting fresh and not failing due to rules and regulations.

The Winspiration Day Association wants to encourage not losing track of one's own life goal and thinking a long time ahead with the certainty that we still have the best before us. This is calming. But it is also everyone's responsibility to handle their freedom with awareness and to design it with courage and morality.

The Portrait

Samy Molcho once asked me: "Why do you do this? Why do you travel once a year to cities, countries and across continents in order to award a prize?" The question was unexpected. It came from a man who has been inspiring people with his charm, humor and knowledge on body language for many decades. Escape from Samy's glances was not possible. So I answered without embellishment: "Extraordinary performance impresses me." He raised his right eyebrow. "But there are Nobel prizes for that." I recognized his intelligent word game, as he pronounced the word "noble, and joined in: "Yes, that's true. Every Nobel Prize winner represents a story of knowledge and research. This is wonderful. But, you know, Samy, with my prize I want to focus a light on men, women and children who improve the world a little with their visions. On people who perform the extraordinary despite physical limitations, strokes of fate or disadvantages. On people who inspire in a wonderful way, who burn with their idea and who tell us again and again through their knowledge and living their dreams: "Discover your capabilities."

I would like to introduce some of them to you on the next pages, some in discussion and some in the form of a portrait. Please follow me.

Professor Muhammad Yunus, Nobel Peace Prize Recipient

„There are poor women all over the world.“

The discussion of whether money makes one happy or not is a verbal exchange among philosophers, entrepreneurs and politicians at a high level. It generally takes place in societies that have the luxury of time and goods in order to enjoy illuminating this topic. Participants in this discussion are well-educated, well-nourished and generally move among others of their ilk. A glance at, for instance, Bangladesh, would make some of them wince and pause and give this discussion another dimension. They would discover: Yes, money can make one happy, because it can change people's fates, even save people's lives, in just small amounts. The economist Muhammad Yunus can tell us a great deal on this topic. He founded the Grameen Bank, has distributed micro-credits to poor people in the country since 1983 and received a Nobel Peace Prize for this in 2006. I met Muhammad Yunus for a conversation which was to encourage reflection on money and happiness:

> *You are saying that we want to eliminate poverty. Is this really possible?*

We can create a world without poverty. The gift that each human being has is unlimited potential, unlimited creativity.

We come packed with it; you cannot separate it out from a human being. But unfortunately we have created a society where many of us never had the opportunity to unwrap that gift. If the society allows me to unwrap that gift I won't be poor, because I know I have the talent and I have the creativity and I pull myself up.

But I also see that there is a lot of people who are stuck in poverty. Sometimes they have a hard time to go out and see the picture. So there is something that we need to change in the paradigm, the poor need to change something and the rich ones, the haves, need to change something.

Most of the change must come from the outside, since poverty is imposed from the outside. Poverty is not created by the poor people, but it is created by the system, by the institutions, by the policies, by the conceptualization of things around us. So we need to change those things. I often say that the seed of poverty is in the institution. Why has it to remain busy with the rich only? We can create a financial institution completely differently, when even the beggars can go out and find the financial services. We didn't come in blank...

No, you proved it.

We do it all the time. This is nothing fancy, nothing utopian. This is our daily bread, this is what we do. But still the banking system has still not changed. And today we created that big crisis.

Where you are involved in schools, do you have special education programs for the kids just to change the paradigms?

Absolutely; when you are trying to change the system, that's where the system begins – in your mind. So the educational system has to adjust to these changes that we are trying to bring in and to the concepts and we must share those concepts with the young people.

Then I talk about the concepts of business, for example. The only concept of business we have in the capitalist economic theory is to make money, as if a human being is a money-making machine. I say human beings are not one-dimensional beings; they are multi-dimensional beings. In order to justify the multi-dimensional view of human being, I often say that we at least need to introduce another type of business into the theoretical framework – this will be to do good to others rather than only benefitting myself. That's what I'm calling social business.

When we have the profit-making business and social business in the same marketplace, what will be different? We will be teaching our young people that you have a choice. The young people can decide or do both – what's wrong with it? They can make money here and use the money to do this. So that's what we are telling the young people. I ask those young people to figure out what type of world they would create. After all, you are not just a passenger on this spaceship. No, they are the pilot of this spaceship. Design the destination where it shall take you and then work for it! Go and do it. Today, young people are given the task.

Young people are taught in minute details how to run a business, but a business for what? Which destination do I want to reach? What do I want to leave behind, when I leave this planet? Today everybody is so busy.

It looks like we came from another planet to Earth to plunder it. Let's plunder it, until everything is exhausted, and then to go home to the other planet. But there is no other home. This is our home. People forget it. And our responsibility is to make it a beautiful home which we can hand over to the next generation. Then it will be our home. We live as if we were the last generation on this planet and did not need to worry about it at all.

You were just talking about companies that are only looking for money. It is nice to make money, but we are making a lot of money today with businesses that are destroying rather than creating something good. We are addicted to the speed of growth, and it's like cancer. The stupidity is that, if the cancer grows big enough, it kills the host. We have no quality really in our gross national product. So, in future I think all what we really need should be a social business and what is more luxury should be the money-making business.

Exactly. You described it very well by using the word "addiction". Making money I understand as a means, but somehow it became an end by itself, as if that was the end result of life. It is not the end result of life. We make money for a purpose. Social business provides me that end —make money and use the money to create the world that I have in my dream. That's what I want to do. And I move piece by piece and I leave my signature on this planet: I was here and this is what I did. All human beings want to leave behind their signature – that I was here and this is my contribution. Maybe it was only a small one, but I did this, no matter what my capacity is, I did my best. If every one of us did that just that little piece the world would be such a better place. Today we've forgotten all of that, as if happiness means what a stack of money you are sitting on.

The stack of money doesn't give you happiness. Happiness is about what you contribute, what difference you make in the life of people and the planet. Our young people are not taught that way. Our young people are taught that it is about getting a good education so they can work for a good company and make good money. Or you can run a good company and make a lot of money for yourself. To do what? How many cars can you own? How many houses can you buy? It doesn't make sense.

So today, we have to get out of that narrow interpretation, of that very narrow interpretation of life and the economic system. Growth by itself doesn't do anything to me; growth is for a purpose, to go somewhere. Otherwise why do we need that?

With your bank, you found out that it seemed to be easier to get this understanding with women. So what is harder with men? Is there a reason why it was easier with women?

The reason why we focused on women comes from something else.

It's a battle that I began with the conventional banks. I was complaining, I was making accusations to them, before I began my work, that they are wrong by rejecting the poor people. And then I said, they are also wrong and unjust that they reject women. Even if she is a rich woman they don't pay any attention. To demonstrate that I was counting their numbers, I said: Look at your numbers. Not even one percent of the borrowers that you have happen to be women.

When I began I wanted to make sure that half of the borrowers in my program were women. My struggle began there. They were scared about money and about going into business. They would say, give it to my husband!

Then, after six years we came to that level of 50-50. Then we noticed that money going to the woman was bringing so much more benefit to the family than the same amount of money going to the man. So, repeatedly, we changed our policy and said, let's focus on women, because it brings so much more benefit to the family. Today, 97 percent of our borrowers are women. We have seven-and-a half million borrowers and 97 percent are women. The bank is owned by the borrowers, which means it is owned by the poor women. So, when micro-credit became a system and spread outside the borders of Bangladesh – it almost became synonymous, micro-credit as a credit for poor women. It's for hundred percent of women around the world.

We see we have a great example, but we still have to learn a lot. Is there some sort of consultancy, if someone wants to set up a social business and learn? Or is it just the books? Can they contact someone like you and say, I want to learn it and can you support us?

Yes, always welcome. We are trained to explain to the people, since we feel very strongly that this is what is needed for the world. In many countries, people are going into debates, intellectual debates and say: "Our country is not the same as Bangladesh. Our people are not as poor as in Bangladesh. Our people are not as trustworthy as people in Bangladesh. There one can lend money without collateral; we can't do that." And I say: "Everything is wrong what you are saying." People are people, no matter where they live. The people are at the very bottom because of the system that pushed them into that situation and you can resolve the situation by removing the hurdle."

Thank you very much, Professor Muhammad Yunus.

Dagmar Riedel-Breidenstein, Ambassador for Tolerance

Suppression in the name of honor

Hatun Sürücü dies on February 5, 2005. She collapses in bright daylight at the Berlin-Tempelhof bus stop, hit by three shots to the head. Her brother is her murderer. A cry of horror is heard through politics and society. It is rare that aggression in Muslim families is revealed so ruthlessly.

The young woman wanted to break away, refuse an arranged marriage, lead a life of self-determination. The so-called honor killing wiped out her wishes and yearnings with a single blow. And since then the violation of this human right has a face. It is modern and beautiful. How greatly everyone wishes that Hatun Sürücü had been allowed to shape her future as wife and mother together with the profession of electrical engineer.

While politicians and experts on Islam debate, while they put coercion, abuse and suppression in immigrant families on their agenda, one Berlin woman takes action. She focuses exactly there were the suffering arises: the guardians of female sexuality, the brothers. The sociologist, Dagmar Riedel-Breidenstein, has considerable experience in conflict resolution. She has headed the Strohhalm (straw) Association for the past twenty years, which acts on behalf of the most vulnerable in our society, the children. The authoritarian attitude of certain immigrant environments towards women was enough reason for her to found "Heroes" in 2007. Since then she has been dedicated to tolerance, to the peaceful co-existence of cultures. Her association is exemplary and has earned respect well beyond the borders of Berlin. With "Heroes" she wants to bring the ideas of freedom and appreciation to immigrant families, to effect a change together. And in order to achieve this goal, she works together with the sons and at times also the daughters.

Breaking down traditions

Dagmar Riedel-Breidenstein and her team offer young men between the ages of 16 and 24 the experience of learning in seminars how women feel when they are suppressed. In role play they feel how hatred makes one helpless. They learn to redefine honor during one year of companionship. For honor is not shown by coercing their sisters. There is only one place for the honor of the man, they learn. At the end the young men stand up in the room and say, with a completely new self-image: "Honor is within me." This focus allows them to open up perspectives far away from control and towards their own life goals. This sentence makes them mild and ready to talk and permits respect for others.

"At the beginning, when we started the project, we were afraid that we would not find enough men from honor cultures for our training and workshops. But this was completely groundless. Young men seek us out on their own. They are curious and feel that something is not right with the old traditions that their fathers preach." Dagmar Riedel-Breidenstein looks around in the group. The men next to her nod and add that it is high time that a future of equality is formed. Some of their mothers and fathers, however, were against the "Heroes" training. "But", says the founder of "Heroes", "they also felt the courage of their sons. They no longer hid behind yelling and threatening. They started to understand women and girls. The atmosphere in the family changed. New thoughts were followed by new behaviors. And they in turn had a positive effect on relationships in the neighborhood. There was another side effect: their sons suddenly had fewer problems at school." Dagmar Riedel-Breidenstein adds enthusiastically: "It is a terrific achievement that the young men are accomplishing during their education. A true transformation is taking place. I am touched when we celebrate the graduation of a year of education in Neukölln, when prominent personalities hand them their certificate. This authorizes the young men to speak at schools as role models."

The Price of Courage

I am touched by this dedication in Berlin. By chance I saw the work of Dagmar Riedel-Breidenstein and her team on television. I was roaming through the channels one afternoon and stopped at a prize award ceremony for this exemplary integration project. I became curious. I researched the work and goals of "Heroes". Ultimately I was convinced that this commitment to equality and appreciation, to tolerance in society, deserved the Winspiration Day Award 2010.

Dagmar Riedel-Breidenstein accepts the award for distinction from the audience and assures them that it will occupy a place of honor. Since then the trophy has been standing on a special shelf and it has a special significance for the heroes of Berlin. It symbolizes the idea that the future can be good, if people follow their goals together in peace. "I like to look back at the award ceremony, at the philosophy of the Winspiration Day: to be pro-active, to move something and not stay in the same old rut. This prize symbolizes the future and prospects and raises the renown of our association." She smiles with satisfaction. She has achieved a great deal in the past six years since the foundation of "Heroes". Each young man she looked after has meanwhile received a technical training diploma and found a profession he likes. Some of them are also working as mentors and moderators in "Heroes" workshops in schools and leisure facilities. "Honor is within us" – this sentence is a promise of tolerance.

One can only hope that this exemplary project does not fail for lack of funds: "The applause of important personalities such as Queen Silvia of Sweden, actors and politicians unfortunately does not change anything about the fact that the Berlin Heroes need both recognition and money in order to continue to fight for human rights. Those who look Dagmar Riedel-Breidenstein in the eye can guess her motto on this topic: "Many paths lead to a life goal. We believe firmly in us and our task in the spirit of the Winspiration Days."

Joana Zimmer,
Singer

Yearning in her voice

In 2006 Joana Zimmer receives the Winspiration Day Award. She is at the top of the charts. She reached no. 2 in Germany with her song "I believe"; appearances on the international stage followed. She was honored for her performance and her impressive path to this performance in Baden-Baden.

When Joana Zimmer stands in the limelight, concentrates and raises her voice, she appears both fragile and strong at the same time. She is submerged in her song, but present nevertheless. She sings her way into the hearts of the audience. They hold their breath and sense the yearning, the courage and the confidence of this young woman, as well as her talent.

Everyone in the hall in these minutes may follow the words that I chose for my introduction: "Joana Zimmer is a woman who cannot be stopped by anyone or anybody, who achieves her dreams with unusual strength, diligence and an unshakable faith in herself."

Joana Zimmer is blind.

> *What does the Winspiration Day Award mean to you today, seven years later?*

It is one of my most important prizes. Since then I have received several awards, including golden records for chart rankings and sales figures. I am happy and proud to receive them. But the Winspiration Day Award is different. It focuses on people, their fate and their calling. I enjoyed it quietly.

What do you connect today with the 7th of May, Winspiration Day?

The idea of reflecting on one's own strength one day a year still makes me enthusiastic. We can move so much. We can take people with us. We can send a message to the world that tells about opportunities. If I can contribute a bit to this with my music, it makes me happy. How often we are confronted by a task and shrink from it. This is a pity. It doesn't get us anywhere. I think that, no matter how trivial the task, one should take care of it with élan and enthusiasm and always with conviction. Success consists of small steps. Success does not come overnight. But every day we get a step closer to success, if we believe in ourselves and do not let hurdles stop us.

Are you always enthusiastic about your tasks?

Yes. I have never refused an assignment. Because I value my success. I am humbled by it. And I feel love; I am grateful for that, too. The people who accompany me, who make an effort for me – I don't want to disappoint them. I want to give back a lot, because I receive a lot. I have a great team. We are one. And that, too, spurs me on.

What does success mean to you?

I was excited when I had my first international appearance. But deep inside I also thought that now finally, after years of hope and persistence, I was getting something back. I dreamed of becoming a singer early on. When I heard Barbra Streisand in "Yentl" when I was 13, this was a key moment. I knew that I wanted to touch people with music. And when I received the Winspiration Day Award, I thought about this wish from childhood. Not glamour and the red carpet are important to me, but inspiration and, beyond that, achieving my goal.

You also run marathons...

Yes, this is similar. If one really wants to progress, there is only one strategy: approaching one's goal with light steps and long breaths. I trained for half a year in order to achieve this task in Berlin. And I learned that I behave the same on the track as in real life. I don't think about the miles. I absolutely want to reach the home stretch, but I approach it step by step. It is the same with my career.

Have you always had this attitude?

I was raised very independently. I am a child of the eighties. My parents lived unconventionally, they weren't married, and they had their own design of life. They did not place a high value on following the beaten track. But they did value order and reliable structures. My parents always carried me close to them as a baby. I think this is good. It warms the baby and makes it feel secure. It strengthens one's trust in the world. If you experience love and trust as a child, you can always carry this within you. It is a huge gift. There are so many people who have everything, but succeed at little.

You were educated in a boarding school. How was this time for you?

I liked it. When I met my choir leader again and she said that I had been so cute earlier with my braids and timid glance, it was like coming home. She was able to use me for all pitches in the choir by the way. We laughed about that. But back to boarding school: my days were filled with singing, sports, learning, shopping and organization. This has shaped me to this very day. I also learned that order is part of life. And taking the easy way doesn't get you far. It is better to climb the stairs than take the elevator. Now I believe that elasticity and strength of purpose are the pillars of success. In both sports and business.

Has success changed you?

No. I see what I can give other people due to my story alone. So I also see my success as a type of duty to give other people courage and to say: You can make it if you believe in yourself and are diligent and work on yourself. Everyone can transform a hindrance into an opportunity. This is what Winspiration Day is about and this is also my motto. And another thing: sudden success can disappear just as suddenly. I know this, so the attention does not affect me adversely.

What are you concentrating on at the moment?

I am writing my first book. I may be young, but I have a lot to talk about.

Thank you, Joana Zimmer.

http://may7.org/xcvw – Joana Zimmer receiving the Winspiration Day Award

Maren Opfermann, World Champion in Gym Wheel Gymnastics

Strength and elegance at a high level

Maren Opfermann was never happy with the either-or mentality in school. She winces when she thinks of the repressive doctrines that children hear every day: "Either you get good grades or you are not among the best, do not belong in the first row". Maren believes: "It is about so much more than these figures on paper, which reveal almost nothing about the child and its dreams. They only show performance in a standardized program. They actually prevent one from seeing talent."

Maren Opfermann freed herself early from these restrictions, made her own goals and creatively designed the steps to achieve them. She learned how to have teachers supervise her, but at the same time to perfect her autodidactic sense. "When I was six, I realized: First I need a goal and then I'll find a way. Earlier this involved small wishes, but over time they grew. At age 15 I wrote this greeting in my cell phone: „I will be World Champion in Gym Wheel Gymnastics.'" – Three years later Maren Opfermann was standing at the very top of the victor's steps, holding her medal and could have hugged the world from happiness. And pride.

Getting up and carrying on

Today Maren Opfermann is one of the youngest public speakers in Germany and Switzerland. She trains gymnasts of both genders. She coaches young people on the road to success. And she knows: Success only feels good when combined with one's talents. Diligence and the will to always get up again and carry on accumulate for this purpose: "A young person learns this in sports. When I fell performing the back somersault and hit my face on the floor of the hall, my head hurt. I could have cried. But I stood up, gritted my teeth and continued training. Why? I had a goal. I wanted to be World Champion in Gym Wheel Gymnastics. Any hesitation would have jeopardized this vision." Neither bruises nor a lack of free time could keep this young woman from turning the greeting on her cell phone into reality. Maren knows that children need goals, big goals, that do not end with getting good grades.

Children want to learn and perform. They need teachers with values who provide inspiration and promise again and again: "If you really want something, your dreams will come true." But in front of excellence the gods immortal have put sweat. Often Maren comforts the gymnasts in her squad at the end of a training session. Because they are afraid of failing to reach their goal. Because they doubt whether they can repeat their performance in competition to the dot. Then she smiles, refreshingly, broadly and openly: "There's no giving up. No excuses. After a defeat you just get up again – and win the next time." She speaks from experience. Although, there will be no more championship in gym wheel gymnastics for her. After having qualified in 2012, she knew: "It's enough.

It's time for a new goal." Decisiveness, too, is one of her strengths. Maren Opfermann learned this many years ago in Kids Coaching with Wolfgang Sonnenburg and Bob Proctor. He encouraged her at the time, far from school and the pressure of teachers, to listen to her inner voice and identify her roadmap in life. She can recall this experience. It helps her during decision-making phases. Maren remembers the moving moment when she entered the stage in Baden-Baden in 2006 with many other young people and called to the parents in the audience: "We feel good and know what we want: just to be ourselves, to be loved as we are."

The sentence for the future blinks on her iPad: in a thousand days, Maren Opfermann will own the horse that she rides every day. Then she will gallop across country bareback and without a bridle. She will hug the horse's neck and feel the kick of freedom. She will talk about this at international events, in front of employees in large companies, in Kids Coaching by the Win-Win AG. The world champion could not present a more authentic theme than "Setting and achieving goals." She is an example. We applaud her.

Wiebke Sohst,
Author of Children's Books

Trip to Tierra del Fuego

Somewhere between the southernmost tip of Latin America and North Alaska is a light-house. It is high and round. Its red and white striped façade shows deep grooves dug by wind and waves over hundreds of years. This tower sends its light rays into the sky and shows seafarers the way. Just like all the other light-houses on the coasts of the sea. But this one is unlike all the others – it is special.

The author Wiebke Sohst traveled there. She departed for Chile and beyond to the Tierra del Fuego over the Magellan Straits. She traveled to the very last tip of the meridian at which Chile and Argentina meet. She crossed rain forests and semi-deserts to Puerto Williams and a little bit farther. The road there was shaped by wonder, by fascination with rare flora and fauna that she knew only from books. She enjoyed the hospitality of the people, was enthused by their stories. One in particular touched her heart: As she stood in front of that old light-house the islanders whispered to her: "It is precisely here, at this point – the end of the world." "Yes, and where does the world begin?" she asked with a laugh. Her new friends didn't know the answer. They shrugged their shoulders. From this point onwards Wiebke Sohst knew that she would write a book, a children's book, that talks about a journey to the end of the world and beyond to its beginning. For traveling has been her passion for ages.

To this very day, she seeks opportunities to experience excitement off the beaten track. Whoever has crossed the Amazon, slept in open huts in the jungle, and protected oneself from storms in deserts of West Africa, knows the diversity of this world and wants to inspire to experience adventure.

Wiebke Sohst published her children's book in 2010. She chose a cute skunk as the main character and the title "Tinga's Trip through Tierra del Fuego":

> Tinga tells his friend of this plan: "I want to see forests, lakes and mountains. And of course the ocean. I want to go to the end of the world! And of course also to this mysterious lighthouse. To the King Penguin! I want to ask him where the beginning of the world is. So I am starting on a research trip in other words", Tinga smiled proudly. The friend thought a bit and answered: "Don't you think this is a bit of a tall order for you? You're only a little skunk – don't forget that!"- "Oh, nonsense – little skunk. I am Tinga, the research traveler!" The friend looked at him with wonder. "Tinga, you"re crazy...and very brave."

And the author wants to give its little readers this courage to grow beyond themselves to carry with them. During the reading hour in kindergartens and elementary schools she has a huge inflatable globe float around. And when she points at Tierra del Fuego, where Tinga lives, then the children's eyes grow wide, because they realize in these moments how exciting it is out there. They would love to climb up the steps to the light-house with Tinga. The little seed of courage can become huge, if there are examples.

Bob Proctor has been a role model for the author. His idea of a paradigm shift in life impresses her. When he spoke at the Winspiration Day 2011 in Zurich, she listened together with many hundreds of guests to his theses on breaking out of the old structures. She was inspired and since then has been using these impulses in her work as business psychologist and division director in a large German corporation – with great success. She has viewed many of her big projects with a different, broader vision since then. And she is writing a second book on adventure and friendship, discovering the world.

For Wiebke Sohst, Winspiration Day is a day of the year that spreads curiosity. That deals with courage and confidence. Just as her books do. She will also read aloud this year on May 7th, 2013, and ask: Who wants to go to Tierra del Fuego? Many of her little readers one day, we hope.

Felix Finkbeiner,
Ambassador for the Future

Plants for the future

"Why is so little done for the future of children?" Felix Finkbeiner asked this question six years ago and turned to those responsible – the adults of this world. At the time Felix was nine years old. He asked teachers, neighbors, entrepreneurs. He asked politicians. The response was a shrug of the shoulders. And the story could have stopped there. Given the silence on the part of the adults, most children would have resorted to the hope that everything will be good. But the problems of the future are too enormous for one to close one's eyes. 30,000 people die daily from malnutrition. A billion people live in absolute poverty. And if climate change continues, then the ice of Greenland will melt, and islands will sink into the oceans. Felix would not be the dedicated, smart and, for his age, so intelligent boy, if he had been satisfied with this silence.

He thinks: If It's about formulating hackneyed sentences in contracts, then the adults on the international stage can talk into the storm of flash-bulbs. The sustainability conference, the Kyoto conference, the millennium conference – all are examples of lip service. But the problem is with implementation.

So Felix decided on his own to make the world a bit better. He looked for supporters of children and young people to set signs, to plant trees. At age twelve, he spoke before the United Nations and more recently from the pulpit of the Erlöserkirche in Munich.

▌http://may7.org/gczb – Sermon by Felix Finkbeiner (German)

The adults listen to his words there, applaud and take his last sentence to heart: "Everything will be fine, if we wake up and do the right thing." At this point he raises his polemic pamphlet. He smiles and spreads his youthful faith in the good in people. He hopes that everyone leaves the church with a different awareness after his one-hour speech, with a broad view of climate change and social justice.

How did your idea, today a success story, start?

It wasn't really that spectacular: Six years ago I held a presentation on the climate crisis at school. I already knew a bit about this subject, since a few days before my grandfather had gone through Al Gore's book "An Inconvenient Truth" with me. I also read about the environmental activist, human rights specialist and Nobel Peace Prize Winner Wangari Maathai of course: She planted 30 million trees in 30 years. So I thought: "If women in Africa can do this, then we children can also plant a million trees in every country of the world." I never thought that a global movement would develop from the final sentence of my class presentation: "Let us plant a million trees in every country on earth!"

Then this sentence became the purpose of your movement?

Yes. My teacher had me repeat the sentence in front of pupils, in front of the principal, in front of other schools. And together with the neighboring schools we founded "Plant-for -the-Planet" two months later. Our goal has been since then – we children and young people would like everybody to plant 150 trees, or 1,000 billion trees in total, on this planet. Since then, we children have already planted millions and, with the help of many adults, over 12.5 billion new trees. The world has become greener and healthier as a result. For each tree binds ten kilograms of carbon dioxide a year.

This is your way of demonstrating for the future?

Yes, that too. As long as governments do not realize that fossil fuels should stay where they belong, in fact in the ground, we will resist this with our campaigns. We demonstrate and plant. We show ourselves and stand up for our future. We, that's 100,000 children, who will not be quiet. We talk. With governments, too. We recently signed a joint agreement with the mayors and the premier of the Mexican state of Quintana Roo. 200 million trees are now being planted there – 150 for each citizen. This is quite a success.

Who are your prominent supporters?

In any case Prince Albert. He is our patron. The former Minister of the Environment, Norbert Röttgen, is among our group of friends and on our campaign posters: "Stop Talking. Start Planting." We children keep the mouths of a number of personalities closed. You can see this on our website

www.plant-for-the-planet.org/de/campaign/stop-talking. It's too late for words. Time is getting away from us.

Where does the money for the trees, the campaigns, the events come from?

We don't receive any public funds. Private individuals support us with monthly amounts of five, ten or twenty euro. We find sponsors or, rather, they find us. We want companies to pay a Future Fee, 0.01 percent of sales, as a sustainability contribution for our future. For a year now we have been selling chocolate – really good chocolate. It is also called "The Good Chocolate". When no-one from the chocolate industry wanted to pay the Future Fee, we thought: Let's produce our own chocolate bars in Switzerland, with the best cocoa beans from Ghana and as a fair-trade product. We can plant one tree for every five chocolate bars sold. In the meantime, though, a number of confectionery companies are paying their contribution.

What vision is being followed by "Plant-for-the-Planet"?

We developed a "3-Point Plan for the Rescue of our Future" in consultations that children from over 105 countries participated in:

1. We want every human being to plant 150 trees – that's one thousand billion trees. We want to have achieved this goal by the year 2020. This can be done. This is how long it took America to send the first manned space-ship to the moon.

2. We must leave the fossil fuels in the ground and reduced carbon dioxide emissions to zero by the year 2050. This means – we will use only renewable energy sources and technologies that already exist today.

3. To ensure that the earth does not heat up more than two degrees Centigrade, we may only put in the air a certain

amount of CO2 into the air, in fact, 600 billion tons. If we share this equally through the world population, this is 1.5 tons of CO2 per person per year. Whoever puts in the air more pays those who do less.

And they can spend the money on medical care and feeding poor people. Or they can invest in new technologies.

We want climate justice and social justice. To fight for these these two goals, we educate one another in the children's academies. To date 1700 academies have taken place around the world. There we learn how to give presentations, how networks function, what is important in negotiations, how we design our future and how we can carry the adults with us. The Winspiration Day Association, too, supports this type of learning and sponsors our academies. Since we children received the Winspiration Day Award 2012 for "Plant-for-the-Planet", we know that Wolfgang Sonnenburg is a friend and promoter, that he represents our goals. On the prize award day in Winterthur in Switzerland on which we happened to plant trees in Switzerland to celebrate World Environment Day, we were surprised with the Award. This spurs us on. This shows us that adults are watching and listening and understand us.

What will you be doing on May 7th?

I'll be in school. And for sure, somewhere in the world, children will be meeting and – hopefully together with adults – planting trees. In places designed for this purpose, or even places that are not. This is very simple: dig, water, plant and then nurture.

Do adults smile at your enthusiasm or do they support your goals?

We are taken seriously. Perhaps we have a children's bonus. But when we speak and act, then a lot of people are astonished at how strong we are, how committed we are to the future.

What annoys you most in the behavior of adults?

When some say: "Climate crisis? There is no climate crisis." Then we say: "If we follow the climate scientists and find out in twenty years that they were wrong, then we haven't done anything wrong. But if we follow the climate skeptics and find out in twenty years that they were wrong, then It's too late to save our future."

Do you and your friends sometimes think that the task that you have taken on is a bit too big for you?

A single mosquito cannot impress a rhinoceros, but a thousand mosquitoes can make it change its direction.

Thank you, Felix, and we wish you great success for the future.

Holger Böhm,
Master Maker

Know one's own strengths

Holger Böhm provides consulting to companies and company founders. He develops educational content for craftsmen at the threshold of becoming masters and coaches men and women who want one thing, to identify their own strengths and live accordingly. He sees himself as a partner at eye-level, as a companion on the way during an exciting period of time. His method is based on three pillars: creativity, strength and community.

How do you find the strengths in your clients?

Via a personal conversation. First we take stock. Then I find out using a special questioning technique what talents the client had as a child or when he or she experienced special attention. So this is how we approach the buried strengths. Very emotional moments can arise, which may churn things up, make them sad or happy. The range of feelings always depends on the client's temperament.

Does this mean in a reverse argument: Whoever works according to his strengths is happy?

Whoever makes his profession a calling is a happy person. This flows into all areas of life. This attracts happiness like a magnet. One can identify happy people by their posture, the shine in their eyes, the smile on their faces. They take care of themselves. They keep social contacts. They are healthy. Their thoughts are positive, as is their charisma.

All true insights are triggered by a crisis. Was this the case with you, too?

My own professional path is an example of my thesis: I completed my education in advertising, concluded my business studies with a concentration in marketing and, almost by compulsion, founded an advertising agency. It was very successful. But I realized quickly that generating orders and sending out invoices wasn't enough for me. I didn't want to squeeze my ideas into communication strategies. I looked for a mentor in those days. I entered into a long process and discovered my true strengths – to carry people along and to create good communities. This insight brought about many changes: I sold my agency and changed my profession. Today I am a successful coach and lecturer. I weave in my marketing know-how when dealing with start-up companies or companies in crisis, but I am primarily focused on finding the strengths of my clients.

Does this mean that a good community fosters personal development?

People can achieve much greater things together than as individual fighters. So I bring people together whose strengths complement one another's and whose goals are similar. An enormous power can grow from this.

The Winspiration Day fits with this thesis.

Yes. A performance on a stage that is well moderated, with examples and touching stories, can be a great motivator. But small formats, too, can have a great impact. The sum of ideas, the sum of energies make this day, the 7th of May every year, valuable. I will ask my master pupils at the Chamber of Trade and Commerce in Braunschweig this year: "How can you make your work really fulfilling?" "How can you turn dreams into reality?"

But a day is not enough to make dreams come true. What do you think?

That's correct. But every process begins with a stimulus before the first step follows. Perhaps we need to be accompanied by people who have our best interests in mind. This could be. But we never need skeptics. We need examples. Or a good community. I, therefore, offer conference calls in addition to my coaching lessons. Then we talk about positive developments, significant experiences during the week and our goals. We take every step together.

Tilo Maria Pfefferkorn, Entrepreneur

Success through personal stock-taking

Actually he wanted to be a priest. When other children dreamed of discovering continents as a pilot or captain, Tilo Maria Pfefferkorn saw himself preaching from a pulpit. The spoken word, values that were lived, the reliability of tradition and ritual – all this impressed him. But things turned out differently. He became an entrepreneur. And, according to his understanding of Luther, he established a family, planted a tree and wrote a book. By age 30, these tasks had been accomplished. So he asked himself: what now? Where are there more challenges? He found them as an assistant professor in business administration, as an entrepreneur in a multi-office service with several locations in Hamburg and today the „eco office centers" of Hamburg. Tilo Maria Pfefferkorn is passionate about his tasks and expects the same from his employees.

> *Among other things you accompany students and company founders on their career path. What are your guidelines for success?*

Learning. Life-long learning. And always ask again and again: What can I do really well? Or even better: What do I really love? What tasks fulfill me? Where do I want to devote my strengths? In other words, free up your head from the expectations of others. Listen to yourself with concentration for once in order to figure out what life you really want to live. We have the freedom of drawing our own designs. This is a creative process. But we do not learn this creativity in school or at university, unfortunately. It is missing altogether. But it is decisive to one's own happiness and success.

You promote a subject called creativity in the school schedule?

Absolutely. The focus at school is more on a school sprint rather than finding one's own personality. If I were able to change anything, I would have children go to school at age four. This would give them more time to discover themselves and develop. Four of my five children learned classical Greek after they learned Latin according to the humanistic tradition. At first glance there is not much one can do with this dead language. But at second glance huge potential opens up. The children become quietly absorbed in this task and discover the power of concentration. They learn that creativity grows slowly. It needs space. Almost incidentally they learn what it can mean to do something outside the main stream. I think that many parents and teachers forget to allow their children time to play, to learn, to discover themselves.

And the sprint continues at university?

Yes. And there is another thing that I find fault with: the curricula are obsolete. I note some good approaches, for instance, children are already learning in elementary school how to present a subject to the class – show and tell. This helps them later at university. But on the topic of managing people, about how to deal with one another, they learn almost nothing. The mainspring is alas not to ask like a good pastor: What moves you? What would you like to achieve or change? How would you like to enthuse people later on? Why do you want to do that? Rather, it is: How do I reach my goals as efficiently as possible and earn money as a result? This question is permitted, but it does not make much sense to ask it in cases in which I am doing something that doesn't move me.

So thinking about career and money is wrong?

When I hire a new employee, of course I look at their C.V. and references, but the question of whether the man or woman will fit into my company is a much greater part of the decision. Knowledge is only of secondary interest to me. This can be easily added to. But character, personality, dedication, attitude to life, self-worth and a feeling for happiness, that's what I have to feel. So after an initial interview I give the applicant the book "The Big Five for Life. What really counts in life" and ask him or her to read it and discuss it with me in a later telephone call. I want to learn what moves him. After that I will know whether the tasks will suit, whether personal goals will be fulfilled in this place. And again and again, even if they are not hired, the applicants thank me and say: "I"ve never thought so intensively about myself."

> *The 7th of May, Winspiration Day, is also a day on which people can reflect on themselves and identify their strengths and what visions are guiding them. What do you organize in Hamburg on this day?*

We document happiness. For four weeks we write down an answer every day to the question: "What was the best part of your day?" For: regardless of how stressful the day may have been, we can identify one special, pleasing moment. Because we have them every day. If we focus our view on that, it will stay bright.

Top performance grows better in light and warmth. So we ask an individual every day about his or her best work experience and ask them in turn to ask another. So on the 7th of May there will be many people who can report on their happiness. On the 7th of May we will look back on experiences and developments and events that inspired us on this day and on the path to this day. We notice that there are grandiose moments every day. We will experience gratitude and sharpen our expectations of the good things to come.

What is your personal vision as entrepreneur?

To open up wide playing fields for my customers; to encourage them to design working spaces that are sensible and modern. Not narrowness, but independence and joy in one's work, counts. I want to take away their fear of dealing with freedom. And freedom to me also means – throwing off dead weight, giving up tasks in order to concentrate on the most important, on core competence. I offer results-oriented solutions that I will continue to fine-tune until they suit every single customer with my multi-office service. I want to provide ideas and companionship – to be a reliable innovator in the area of office services. We create free spaces.

Thank you, Mr. Pfefferkorn.

Perspectives –
Thinking ahead with dreams

"People with small dreams will remain small throughout their lives."- Robert T. Kiyosaki

There is a dream that is universal. It covers the longitudes and latitudes of this Earth and fills people with yearning. Regardless of skin color, age or gender, it unites nations across all language barriers. Its stuff is flimsy in consistency, cannot be squeezed into a formula or ordered by law. It can only be fulfilled by thoughts and images that are created in people's heads. I am speaking of happiness.

The great thinkers – philosophers, the literati, artists and natural scientists – attempted to explore happiness, to formulate it as the essence of religions and spiritual history. Intelligent thinking has guided the world since, allowing room for freedom and self-fulfillment. Nevertheless, ever new aspects are added, because each person leaves tracks in life. So the dream of happiness will never end, from birth to death, and then it will start again from the beginning in the next generation. Defining happiness remains an ongoing task that everybody has to undertake on his own, so that at the end he can say: "Life was good. I have no regrets."

So that we have no regrets at the end

In 1968 Robert F. Kennedy stood before the students of the University of Kansas and caused concern among his audience: "Our gross national product is now 800 billion dollars a year. But this gross national product includes air pollution and cigarette advertising and ambulances that remove the consequences of bloodbaths on our highways. It includes special locks for our front doors and the prisons for those who break into our front doors. It includes the destruction of giant redwoods and the decimation of our natural wonders due to chaotic urban sprawl. [...] But our gross national product does not take into account the health of our children, the quality of their education or their joy in playing. It does not include the beauty of our poetry or the strength of our marriages, the intelligence of our public debates or the integrity of our civil servants. It does not measure either our common sense or our courage, our wisdom or our education, our compassion or our devotion to our country. In short, it measures everything but what makes life worth living."

Where is the courage to uphold the themes of happiness and to drive out the greatest hindrances to this happiness – fear and doubt? When Martin Luther King issued a call for a non-violent movement against the discrimination against blacks, his followers were the greatest hurdle. They had experienced suffering and suppression for too long. They doubted that everything would ever get better. 40 years later the US elected its first black President.

The world is turning towards the good. We must only perceive this and accelerate it with our energy. We can demand from politicians that they weave the enormous wealth of medical and technical knowledge into everyday matters, rather than allowing obstructive lobbyists space or stirring up fears that jobs could disappear. This doom saying is completely misplaced. One thing is sure, though: In the future tasks and demands will change. This is a good thing, since it offers new perspectives.

Influential economists preach that attention should be directed towards people and their satisfaction rather than a welter of products and a focus on profits. The great, really great, players have understood the secret that happy employees give of their best.

It is often the companies that combine tradition and innovation that ask themselves constantly: How can we adapt our products to requirements; how can we eliminate defects? 90 years ago, Otto Bock wanted to facilitate the lives of the war-wounded with his wooden prostheses. Nowadays the company provides high-tech prostheses from fiber composite materials borrowed from the aviation industry: Heinrich Popow sprinted to a 100 meter victory in London with Otto Bock's prosthetic leg. He became a model for a whole generation. McDonalds has changed its nutritional guidelines: armed with the knowledge of poor nutrition offered by fast food, the company is now relying on bio foods. And the founder of the dm-drogeriemark drugstore chain, Götz W. Werner, with his employee-friendly philosophy and meticulous business ethics is setting standards that should provide an example to many. World renowned managers are still amazed at the modern approaches in Semco of Brazil, the machine manufacturer: Employees elect their bosses, determine their jobs and tasks and even their salaries. They are applying business doctrines in topsy-turvy fashion and yet performance is strong.

We yearn for awareness images for our abilities and for business models that foster employees beyond all measure. Then we can abolish the petty brainstorming of politicians on the minimum basic security of citizens to where it belongs: in a cabaret program.

A Bonsai can grow

No-one should have the right to keep a person small just as those Japanese trees which are cultivated in mini-format. A bonsai, too, can grow if it is no longer supported and surrounded by wire. In our society growth starts in kindergarten. Children hunger for knowledge and development by the age of three. We must ensure that best teachers supervise the very smallest in order to show them every day that they can feel and permit emotions, that they can discover themselves with care and freedom in play. Systems of value are created in this early period in life. There will never be a time when they form their character with greater intensity and establish their confidence. Personality developments begin in these first years of life and continues through the phases of being a pupil, student, father or mother, employee, as a contributor to our society.

The Skills of the Future

I don't need to be a psychic to describe the capabilities that will determine careers within the next few years. Experts have defined future skills such as cross-cultural thinking. Countries are coming ever closer not least due to the speed of media. Deep understanding for one another will shape markets in all industries. In addition mathematical intelligence will become established, for new technologies can be beneficial on a day-to-day basis by translating data quantities into specific concepts and comprehensible applications. Adaptive thinking will be in demand, for we need to create solutions rather than complain about problems. And I believe personally that language, whether spoken or in writing, is the symbol of the future. It encourages. It motivates. It maps the dream of happiness with words. It awakens various areas in the brain. I don't mean the self-help books, millions of which are tossed into the market every year and which inflate small theses and ultimately can only present tired methods. We don't need the ten thousandth manual on time management. Rather, I mean texts that transmit a true message, because they inspire and allow us to reflect on our life and on what we want to accomplish with a wink in the history of time.

Accomplishing the Best together

The Winspiration Day Association wants to measure happiness in life together with you, provide life with perspectives. So that at the end we have no regrets, but transmit the best we can achieve to our children. Every individual can contribute according to his discretion and capabilities and on his level. Perhaps a first step is to sit down in peace and quiet, removed from the day's hectic pace. Choose a place that gives you a sense of well-being and write our five personal life goals down. These are your top five. They will lead you through the days and years. Share them with us. We will add them to our formulas for happiness and inspire others. We can move a great deal together. Pero Mićić is correct when he writes: "We need a good relationship to our „Future I" and our ‚Future We'."

As President of the Winspiration Day Association I was able to encounter impressive people. All of them have a message. They are sources of inspiration and true examples, because they contribute a bit to a better world with their actions. They are already thinking about tomorrow today and do not stay mired in the sad positions that our media like to celebrate. They think into the future. Such as Felix Finkbeiner, who has assumed the task of keeping people and nature in harmony together with children from all over the world. Such as Dagmar Riedel-Breidenstein, who makes it clear to young immigrant men how criminal so-called honor killings are. Such as Professor Manfred Spitzer, who shows in his capacity of scientist how learning changes our thinking, in fact, how learning allows the center of happiness in our brain to switch on and release the hormone dopamine. Happiness is fleeting, but can always be invoked by developing one's own capabilities. Such as Muhammad Yunus, who explains: "Do we all want to become beggars? – No. It is better to have people work." It's not about the distribution of charity. It is about helping people to help themselves. Such as Jane McGonial, who invented a digital game on happiness and entered the hearts of hundreds of thousands of men and women. Her directions for happiness are based on the regrets of the dying as published by the nurse Bronnie Ware in her book. McGonial transforms the five important sentences into a competence for the future, directions for happiness. I think they are fitting precisely at this point in the book and they are roughly as follows:

1. Have the courage to live your true self.

2. Connect profession and calling.

3. Show your love, your emotions.

4. Nurture your friendships.

5. Decide to be happy.

From Dream to Reality

The Winspiration Day is designed to place the focus on happiness once a year. I have been initiating this power day since 2003, always on the 7th of May. Since then, people in Germany, the US, Romania, Switzerland and other countries get together. They organize a major show or decide to celebrate quietly, feeling their own potential in a small group. I encourage them to design the future and send an image to the universe by means of presentations, workshops and vision parties. Because I am convinced that once expressed, visualized or even formulated in writing, we can consolidate our thoughts purely on turning our idea for the future into reality. Energy fields will shift towards the positive. Awareness of one's own perspectives on life will grow – I call this Purpose.

Finally I am leaving you with a wish on my part:

Write your politicians specifically about what you expect from them: not more nor less than a framework for happiness as provided for in the Human Development Index. Collect signatures. Organize meetings. Send mailings to people, organizations, enterprises. Give color to your ideas once a year on May 7th. We of the Winspiration Day Association support you.

Thank you for accompanying me to this point. I would like to continue our discussions.

The future is open. You can decide yourself what it will bring you.

Acknowledgments

Stories begin with conversations, with encounters and sometimes with a few lines: in December of 2012 I received an email with an idea for a book. I wish to thank the writer, Gabriele Borgmann, for our cooperation, for adding the words to my thoughts in this text.

The artist Simon Hofer gave graphic life to the philosophy of the Winspiration Day Association. He designed the logo. Thank you.

My thanks also to all those people who participated in the events, who shared their inspiration and visions.

Together we have achieved a great deal. All will be well, if we continue together.

The Author

Wolfgang Sonnenburg is a mentor, speaker, author and thought leader. The former attorney and entrepreneur was the owner of a law office and partner in a tax consultancy firm and a real estate company.

In conjunction with his organizations, Win-Win-AG and the Nikken Network, as well as the Winspiration Day Association, Wolfgang Sonnenburg wants to inspire the business world to look far beyond profits. For him, it is all about thinking for the future, living in the here and now with a sense of tomorrow. He sees human happiness in a holistic approach. His motto is: "Purpose-driven profit". In this approach as a mentor he encourages optimistic thinking and design and the identification and fine-tuning of one's own capabilities.

He describes the core of his philosophy as: "I encourage myself and others to take up our place in life." Only the interplay of education, health, happiness and financial security leads to true well-being.

Wolfgang Sonnenburg established Winspiration Day in 2003 and founded the Winspiration Day Association in 2012 in order to lend the 7th of May, the day to focus on one's own power, significance worldwide.

Winspiration Day 2005: The program on stage in Hotel Estrel in Berlin inspired hundreds of spectators.

Standing ovation for magnificent artists at the end of the show in Berlin 2005

Actress Claudia Wilde has supported the Winspiration Day for many years. In 2005, she joined Wolfgang Sonnenburg on stage.

"Happy Winspiration Day!" Little Rex Lewis is happy about the award and the applause on the big stage in Baden-Baden in 2006.

Singer Joana Zimmer during the final
rehearsal for the Winspiration Day 2005

Sponsor and friend of the Winspiration Day
2010 in Berlin: Dr. Thomas Jäger, Director,
BNI Berlin

Maren Opfermann, world champion in
gym wheel gymnastics first participated in
KidsCoaching. Today she motivates other
young people, as a presenter and trainer,
to achieve their goals in life. In 2010, she
delivered an inpiring speech.

In 2010, professor Manfred Spitzer received
the Winspiration Day Award for his research
into brain-friendly learning.

Ambassador for Tolerance, Dagmar Riedel-Breidenstein, is being honored for her work with the Winspiration Day Award 2010. Together with the "Heroes, she changes the behavior of men with migration background. With that approach she tackles hostility towards women and so-called honor killings.

In 2010, Claudine Krause introduced the youth emergency relief society, Jugendnothilfe Jung und Jetzt e.V. in Berlin. The Winspiration Day Association supported the foundation of this society.

Preparations for the Winspiration Day 2011 in the Renaissance Zürich Hotel

The guests looked forward to a program which would be stimulating and provoke thoughts about one's own dreams in life.

Nicolette du Toit, Marketing Manager, Microsoft Switzerland stepped up for the Winspiration Day 2011 in Zürich and looked forward into the future, with "The New World of Work"

Silence and contemplation in the room: opera singer Fredrik de Jounge captured the audience with his voice.

Pro bycicle racer Franco Marvulli has won many titles: World Champion, Vice World Champion, and Olympic Silver. In 2011, he stood on stage on Winspiration Day.

Finalist of the Swiss Talent Show, Julia Star, sang and set the audience as well as the guests on stage on fire with her youthful spark.

Bob Proctor travelled all the way from Canada. For many years he has been a friend and companion of Wolfgang Sonnenburg, At the Winspiration Day 2011, he delivered a brillant 2-hours workshop, "Create your own Economy.

Ideas with future: Students present their business project at the Winspiration Day 2011 in Zürich. From canvas, they created bags which became very popular. They were branded and have established themselves in the world of fashion under the label "backbord".

At 97 years of age, she still has dreams: Jennet Robins talked about her wishes for life and touched with her esprit many hundreds of spectators. Also after her death in 2012, her book, "A Quest for Love" still remains worthwhile reading. http://may7.org/ebxx

Humor meets beauty: Clown Shiven and Nadine Vinzens, Miss Switzerland 2002/2003, got along perfectly at the Winspiration Day in Zürich.

Made in the USA
San Bernardino, CA
01 July 2016

CONTENTS

Dedication
Acknowledgments
Preface
Introduction

CHAPTER

DEDICATION

To my darling wife, Ruth, who is the essence of love, a personal source of encouragement and inspiration, and a cause for my passionate commitment to excellence in leadership.

To my daughter and son, Charisa and Chairo (Myles Jr.) who continually provide incentive for the exercise and development of my leadership potential.

To the leader in every follower. To the millions who have resolved that they will always be subjugated to the whims of others.

To all the individuals whom I have had the privilege and opportunity to inspire to strive to be all they were born to be.

To the millions of great men and women who presently occupy the womb of some mother, children destined to change the world and become the leaders of destiny.

And to all the Third World peoples, around the world, whose potentials were and in some cases, still are oppressed and suppressed by the opinions and judgements of others.

To all aspiring Leaders for whom life holds such promise.

ACKNOWLEDGMENTS

This work is a synergistic product of many minds. I am forever grateful to the inspiration and wisdom of the many great men and women who, through their commitment to the passion for releasing their potential, have left a legacy to motivate me and my generation.

I am also grateful for the members, friends and colleagues at Bahamas Faith Ministries International, whose faithful prayers, patience and loyalty inspire me and allow me to fulfill my purpose and potential, especially my faithful executive administrator and eldest sister, Sheila Francis.

For the Development and production of this book, I feel a deep sense of gratitude to:

My wonderful wife, Ruth, and our children, for their patience, understanding and support during my many travels and involvements outside the home. You make it easy to fulfill God's will.

My close circle of friends, pastors and board members-Richard Pinder (my friend and in-law indeed), Henry Francis, Dave Burrows, Wesley Smith and Jay Mullings (the gentle giant whose companionship on the road for many years of travel has contributed to the releasing of my potential)-whose loyalty and commitment to the vision can take credit for most of what God has done in my life.

The best friends in the ministry anyone could ever have: Turnel Nelson, Bertril Baird, Peter Morgan, Fuschia Pickett, Ezekiel Guti, Fred Price, Allen Langstaff, Jerry Horner, Kingsley Fletcher and Richard Dementte.

And finally, to the Source and Supplier of all potential, the Omni-potent One, the Father and Lord of all creation, and His Son, my elder Brother, Jesus Christ, and my personal Counselor, the Holy Spirit. Thanks for the privilege of serving You.

PREFACE

The world is filled with followers, supervisors, and managers but very few leaders. Leadership is like beauty, it's hard to define but you know it when you see it. Time has produced a legacy of distinguished and outstanding individuals who have impacted history and the ongoing development of mankind. These individuals consisted of both men and women, rich and poor, learned and unlearned, trained and untrained. They came from every race, color, language and culture of the world. Many of them had no ambition to become great or renowned. In fact, most of the individuals who have greatly affected mankind were simple people who were victims of circumstances that demanded the hidden qualities of their character, or they were driven by a personal passionate goal.

Leaders are ordinary people who accept or are placed under extraordinary circumstances that bring forth their latent potential, producing a character that inspires the confidence and trust of others. Our world today is in desperate need of such individuals.

William Shakespeare once wrote, "There is a tide in the affairs of men." In these words, he was expressing his observation of the turning pages of history and their influence upon our lives. It's as if we as men and nations are caught in a tide of providential events. There have been eras in the history of our world in which multiple sets of tide-like influences have impacted our civilization and culture at nearly the same time. These historical incidents are known as "crossroads of history." I would suggest that in the twentieth century, we are at a confluence of historic tides.

In the past two decades, a relatively short span of time within this century, the world has experienced many remarkable changes in the realms of science, technology, medicine, space, and hundreds of other so-called advancements in our nations. Strangely, this century has also seen more distressing things than any previous century, devastating wars, monstrous new weapons, countless natural disasters and fatal diseases.

We must agree that our generation lives in a swirling tide of events, dreams, promises, threats and changing ideas about the present and the future. Certainly our century has been the most politically interesting, the bloodiest, the most revolutionary and the most unpredictable of any century in history. This confluence of strange conditions presses this generation to ask anew, "Why am I here? What is the purpose of life? Why are life and reality the way they are?"

The leaders of our time are bewildered when they are called upon to explain the reasons that our world is the way it is, or to suggest a direction for the future. Many in positions of public trust confess that they are just trying to keep the lid on, and others have abandoned even that hope. We need competent leaders.

Added to this bleak environment is the painful reality that over the past few decades there seems to have been a dramatic leadership vacuum developed throughout the world. In every arena there is an absence of quality, effective leadership. In the political, civic, economic, social and spiritual arenas, recent events indicate that previous generations have produced a poor quality of characters who fade in the presence of true leadership and leave our present generation in this same leadership vacuum.

The recent disgrace and fall of many renowned Christian leaders, the exposure of corruption and unethical activities among political leaders, and the covert conspiracies of governments betraying their own people, is evidence that this lack of quality leadership is affecting every sphere of our lives.

It is in this environment that we as stewards of this present age must face the challenge of identifying, developing, training, releasing and reproducing a generation of leaders who would secure the future for our children and their children. "Becoming a Leader" is designed to contribute to this challenge with the hope that you would be inspired to respond to the call of destiny, responsibility, and awaken the potential leader within you.

> *"A good leader not only knows where he is going, but he can inspire others to go with him."*

INTRODUCTION

In every person, there is potential for leadership. Despite this latent ability lying below the surface, there are very few individuals who realize this power and fewer still who have responded effectively to the call. As a result, our nations, societies and communities are suffering from an astounding leadership vacuum.

Everyone deplores this lack of true leadership throughout the world, and the blame usually lands at the feet of the individual who hasn't made the grade. Greed, timidity and lack of vision are rampant among the current crop of **"pseudoleaders."**

Where are the genuine leaders? Where are the individuals who would be willing to take responsibility for the present situation and conditions in the world? Who is willing to accept the challenge, to face it head on with integrity, character and a commitment to execute righteous judgment for a better world? From America to Australia, from China to Chile and from Canada to the Caribbean, the world is in desperate need of true leaders.

Our communities need positive role models, our children need fathers and our world needs direction. Where are the leaders? Who are they? What makes an individual a leader? Who becomes a leader? When does one become a leader?

This is not the first time that an obvious vacuum of quality, effective leadership has prevailed throughout the world. A quick glance at the historical record will show that during periods when moral, social, economic, spiritual and political chaos gripped nations, the greatest leaders in history surfaced. Even the biblical record reveals God's demand for quality leaders during times of human crisis. His search for effective leadership is expressed in numerous statements such as:

But now your kingdom will not endure; the Lord has sought out a man after his own heart and appointed him leader of his people...
(1 Samuel 13:14).

I looked, and there were no people...
(Jeremiah 4:25).

Go up and down the streets of Jerusalem, look around and consider, search through her squares. If you can find but one person who deals honestly and seeks the truth, I will forgive this city. (Jeremiah 5:1).

I look for a man among them who would build up the wall and stand before me in the gap on behalf of the land so I would not have to destroy it, but I found none. (Ezekiel 22:30).

These scriptures reveal that whenever a nation has a lack of quality, legitimate and just leaders, national deterioration occurs. They also reveal that God's remedy to this type of situation is the discovery and raising up of new, trained leaders committed to justice and righteousness. In essence, *quality leadership* is the key to a prosperous and peaceful life and nation.

It is obvious that currently, our nations are painfully in need of such leaders. The church is desperately in need of leaders. Our homes are crying out for leadership. Our youth are begging for leaders. God's answer to all our social, moral and economic problems is qualified, just and righteous leaders. However, it is impossible for an unrighteous world to produce righteous leaders and an unjust system to produce just characters, as it is impossible for a bitter spring to bring forth sweet water.

It is generally accepted that the essence of leadership is the exercise of influence for a common cause. For instance, the command given to the Christian church by Christ is, "Go and make disciples of all nations, teaching them the things I have taught you." This is a direct mandate to provide leadership for nations, instructing them to live according to the principles of the kingdom of God.

This commission clearly places the responsibility for producing the quality leaders that this nation and the world needs upon the shoulders of the Christian church, yet it is sad that even the church itself is in need of quality leadership. Perhaps this is because the focus of the church and its theology has been preoccupied with heaven and preparing individuals to leave the planet, thus forsaking the responsibility of producing quality leaders for our nations. Today, the responsibility to meet this need is the challenge of our generation, for the sake of the generations to come.

By reading this book, you are now responsible to hear the cry in your nation, your city, your community, your church and your family for leaders. You are a candidate for leadership in your generation.

Becoming a leader isn't easy, just as becoming a doctor or poet isn't easy, and anyone who claims otherwise is fooling himself. However, learning to lead is a lot easier than most of us think it is, because each of us possess the capacity for leadership. In fact, every one of us can point to some leadership experience, whether it was in a classroom, a gang, a Sunday school play, as a parent or in responsibility for household chores.

This book is designed to assist you in developing and refining your leadership qualities and to awaken and enhance the potential leader hidden within you. Whatever your leadership experience, it's a good place to start. We cannot function without leaders. Our quality of life depends on the quality of our leaders. And since no one else seems to be volunteering, it's up to you. If you've ever had dreams of leadership, now is the time, this is the place and you're it. We need you. Now, let us proceed together as we unearth the leader hidden within you.

A true leader is a model for his followers.

1

UNDERSTANDING LEADERSHIP

> *"Great leaders never desire to lead but to serve."*

Leadership is the ability to lead others by influence. If this principle holds true, then we have all exercised some degree of leadership in our lives. Maybe the experience wasn't running a company or governing a state, but perhaps it was the influence of one friend on another, or as a parent on a child, a spouse on a family, a teacher on students, a pastor on a congregation, a manager on subordinates or a politician on his constituents. Leadership can also be seen simply as responding to responsibility.

Leadership has very little to do with what you do and is fundamentally a matter of becoming who you are.

Therefore, if you have ever been given any measure of responsibility, whether it was to run an errand for your parents, restore order to the kitchen after a family meal, make a presentation before a class, clean the restrooms in a church, organize an event or reorganize your bedroom, in each case you were exercising some measure of leadership skills.

I know you may have never considered some of the above activities as relating to such a technical subject as leadership, however, it is perhaps your very concept of leadership that prevents you from becoming the leader you were born to be. Furthermore, it is essential to note that all the above activities are functions of behavior and are not elements of character. In essence, you will learn throughout this book that leadership has very little to do with what you do and is fundamentally a matter of becoming who you are.

THE GREAT LEADERSHIP MISCONCEPTION

The great Greek philosophers such as Plato, Aristotle, and Socrates considered and explored the dynamics of human behavior and the nature of humanity. A significant portion of their investigative contemplation focused on the art and the dynamics of human social relationships as they relate to governing. They addressed the subject of leadership and examined in much detail this complex issue.

One of their basic conclusions and tenets was that leadership is a product of natural endowment and traits of personality. In essence, one is born to lead while others are born to follow and be subordinate. For many years now, this concept of leadership has prevailed in numerous schools of thought and has gone for the most part, unchallenged. The results have produced a historical, global concept that the masses are destined to be ruled by the significant privileged few, sentenced by providence to their circumstances, to live life as dictated.

However, time and time again, history has presented us with case studies that contradict the premise of this perception of leadership, and in many ways defy the notion that leaders are "born." Countless deposed kings and hapless heirs to great fortunes can attest that true leaders are not born, but made. It's as if true leaders invent themselves. They are not made in a single weekend seminar, as many of the leadership-theory spokesmen claim.

Billions of dollars are spent annually by and on would-be leaders. Many major corporations offer leadership development courses. However, I believe more leaders have been made by accident, circumstances, sheer grit or determination than have been made by all the leadership courses put together. Leadership courses can only teach skills. They cannot teach character or vision. Developing character and vision is the way leaders are made. Leaders are not gifts but results.

There are individuals who, based on Plato's theory would never have been accepted as leadership material, and yet became some of the greatest leaders in history. Moses, a fugitive from Pharaoh's justice, a murderer and a man who presented every excuse why he should not be considered for leadership, became the greatest lawgiver in history.

Gideon, the Hebrew coward, was threshing wheat for his farmer-father when the call came for him to rise and become the deliverer of his nation. His response to this challenge was, "My clan is the weakest, my family is poor and I am the least likely candidate in my family." Yet Gideon became one of the greatest leaders and warriors of his generation.

David, an insignificant shepherd boy who was considered the least in his family, has his place in history as the greatest king the nation of Israel has ever produced. Peter, a simple fisherman, was catapulted to the position of the first major leader of the early Christian church.

The Great Depression was the crucible in which Franklin D. Roosevelt was transformed from politician to leader. Harry S. Truman became president when Roosevelt died, but it was sheer grit that made him a leader. Dwight D. Eisenhower, America's only five-star general, was underestimated by his contemporaries and turned out to be his own man, and a great leader.

Perhaps, lying deep within you, buried by the misconception that only special people are called to the lofty position of leader, is one of the greatest leaders of our time. I believe there is a leader in everyone waiting to serve his or her generation. It is important that you change your concept of leadership now and see yourself the way your Creator sees you. We are not all the same, but we are all leaders in our own unique way.

EVERYONE CAN LEAD

Learning to lead is a lot easier than most of us think it is, because each of us has the capacity for leadership. *Leaders are simply people who dare to be themselves and are able to express themselves fully.* By this I mean that they know who they are, what their strengths and weaknesses are, and how to fully deploy their strengths and compensate for their weaknesses. They also know what they want, why they want it and how to communicate what they want to others. They know how to achieve their goals.

To a leader, life is a career.

To a leader, life is a career. You become a leader when you decide not to be a copy but an original. In essence, a leader does not set out to be a leader per se, but rather to maximize himself fully and freely. True leaders have no interest in themselves or vying for a position, but an abiding interest in expressing themselves. The leader within you comes alive when you discover the purpose and vision for your life, and set out to fulfill it without compromise.

Although I have said that everyone has the capacity

for leadership, I am sad to say that I do not believe everyone will become a leader, especially in the confusing and antagonistic context in which we live. Too many people are mere products of their circumstances and victims of their social context. They lack the will to change, to develop their potential and declare independence from the opinions of others. Becoming a leader is synonymous with becoming yourself. It's that simple and that difficult.

CREATED TO LEAD

Do you remember the last time you were commanded to do something or ordered to do something? Can you recall the natural inclination deep within you to resist the demand even though you cooperated? This natural desire to rebel against orders or commands can be seen in the smallest child and stays with us throughout our lives. As adults however, we have developed sophisticated behavior mechanisms to regulate and control this urge. What is the source of this desire to resist the spirit of domination of our person? Why do we all hate to be told what to do?

**You become a leader when you decide
not to be a copy but an original.**

To answer these questions, one must go back to the beginning and the creation of man. The scriptures record that in the beginning, God created the heavens and the earth and fashioned everything to sustain life. Then in Genesis 1:26-28 we find these words:

"Then God said, 'Let us make man in our image, in our likeness, and let them rule over the fish of the sea and the birds of the air, over the livestock, over all the earth, and over all the creatures that moves along the ground.' So God created man in his own image, in the image of God he created him; male and female he created them. God blessed them and said to them, 'Rule over every living creature."

Here in these statements lies the heart of the purpose for man's creation and the key to his nature. To understand yourself, you must understand the principles established in these words. First, it is essential to note that God created us "IN HIS IMAGE AND LIKENESS." These words connote His authority, character and his moral and spiritual nature. God's nature is one of power and rulership. He refers to himself as the "King and Ruler of the Universe." Therefore, deeply embedded in the nature of man is the spirit of rulership and authority. Secondly, God established man's role and function in relationship to the earth by stating, "LET THEM RULE OVER ALL THE EARTH." This declaration confirms his ordination of the following principles:

A)   God created man to have dominion over the earth.

B)   God gave dominion over the earth to both male and female.

C)   He never gave man the authority to dominate one another.

The male is not to dominate the female, and vise versa.

D)   He specified what they were to dominate . . ."the earth and creation."

E)   They were created to dominate and not be dominated.

These principles are fundamental to our very nature and fulfillment. If we were created for the purpose of dominion, then we are designed to fulfill this purpose and will never be personally satisfied until we are performing this responsibility. We must also have a clear understanding of what it means to dominate.

This word **dominate** has different shades of meaning which include, **rule**, **manage**, **control**, **dictate**, **subject**, **influence**, **lead**, **keep under control**, **govern**, **command**, **to master**, **have power over and to have authority**. These words are all pregnant with the concept of leadership and all describe God's purpose for your life. In essence, God created all of us to rule, govern, control and influence the earth. He created all of us to lead. There is a leader in everyone waiting to be released. You were never created to be dominated.

This is why whenever the human spirit is dominated by another human, whether it is by a governing system or forced labor, there is a natural, inevitable desire and will to throw off this unnatural restraint. This means that in God's original plan and purpose, he never intended for there to be any followers and subordinates among men as we know it today.

In essence, God created all of us to rule, govern, control and influence the earth. He created all of us to lead.

In essence, God created all of us to rule, govern, control and influence the earth. He created all of us to lead. They were all intended to exercise His authority and dominion as a corporate entity on earth, displaying His power, wisdom, influence and glory. We were designed to be subjected only to His Spirit, which would rule in our hearts and thus establish self-government.

This principle is also seen in God's assignment to the first man in the garden. His first command to the man was "work." This assignment was not accompanied by any supervisors, managers or bosses to oversee man's responsibilities. He was only accountable to God. In essence, man's accountability for the task assigned him was direct to God, and not another man.

"You were never created to be dominated."

This aspect of direct leadership responsibility is also expressed in God's response to the nation of Israel after he had delivered them from the hand of Egyptian oppression and brought them unto himself in the Sinai desert. He told them they would be his people and He would be their God. However, the effect of the oppression had taken such a toll on their ability to take responsibility for their lives, that they still felt the need to have the physical domination of a human over them in order to function.

Therefore, they cried out for a king. God's response to their request was a surprise. He attempted to discourage them from setting up a human ruler, and declared his desire to be the direct authority in their lives. He said, "I will be your God and you will be my people."

However, after their insistence, he granted them their request but strongly warned them of the danger-ous consequences of having another man dominate their capacity for leadership. It is important to note that this does not and should not imply that God designed mankind to have a chaotic society without accountability to each other or without subjection to authority.

On the contrary, He, being a God of excellence, created everything to function in decency and order with each component and person fulfilling his unique part in the whole. Each being responsible for leader-ship in his sphere of assignment, accountable ultimately to God the creator. In other words, each man is a leader created to be led by the Spirit of God! No one is to lord over another or dominate the other's abilities and potential to maximize himself.

However, as a result of man's disobedience, rebellion and his subsequent fall from grace, the Spirit of God was removed from man's spirit, leaving him at the mercy of his external environment. This led to the need and establishment of external governing in order to restrain mankind from unchecked abuse of his powers and authority. Consequently, the relationship of leader and follower, ruler and the ruled, supervisor and the supervised, master and the mastered was established.

Evidence of this interruption in God's purpose and plan for man to exercise leadership is underscored in the pronouncements he made to the man and the woman after their disobedience to his word.

To the woman he said, 'Your desire will be for your husband, and he will rule over you.' To Adam he said, 'Cursed is the ground because of you; through painful toil you will eat of it all the days of your life. It will produce thorns and thistles for you...By the sweat of your brow you will eat your food.' (Gen. 3:16-19)

Here we see the reversal of the order of dominion and authority. Instead of both man and woman ruling and dominating the earth together as was

God's original command, the subjection of man over man is introduced. Also, instead of man dominating the earth as was formally established, the earth is now set to dominate man.

This relationship is not natural and therefore goes against our nature to rule, rather than be ruled. In other words, we are all born leaders, created to lead. It is for this reason that God's plan for the human race is to restore his Holy Spirit back to man and thus restore self-government.

If we want effective, just and qualified leaders in our world today, we must look to God to raise up men and women who are filled with his spirit and led by his will.

> **We are all capable of leadership by design, but we cannot lead correctly and effectively unless we are led by his Spirit.**

Just like an automobile that was created to operate on gasoline, if it is not fitted with this necessary source of energy supply, it is unable to perform its purpose. If its tank is filled with water instead of gasoline, the vehicle will malfunction and eventually destroy it's vital parts. This is the condition of mankind since the fall. We were created to operate by the Spirit of God. Therefore, if any other spirit possesses or influences our lives, we are unable to become or function as the leaders we were created to be.

UNDERSTANDING LEADERSHIP

I challenge you to step forward ar
the nation and community in w
restore Godly, just, effective and spi
to the world by first submitting yourself to the Supreme Leader and Creator of Leaders.

Send some men...one of its leaders.
(Numbers 13:2)

Good leadership is indispensable.

PRINCIPLES

1. Leadership is the ability of one person to influence others.

2. Leadership has very little to do with WHAT YOU DO and is fundamentally a matter of BECOMING WHO YOU ARE.

3. Developing character and vision is the way leaders are made. Leaders are not gifts but results.

4. It is important that you change your concept of leadership now and see yourself the way your Creator sees you.

5. God created all of us to rule, govern, control and influence the earth.

6. Each man is a leader, created to be led by the Spirit of God.

2

WHAT IS LEADERSHIP?

"Leadership is first being, then doing. It is the ability to inspire others to become and fulfill themselves by you doing the same."

Leadership by definition is simple and yet complex. For hundreds of years studies have been done to determine what is leadership and what makes one a leader. The results are as varied as the attempts to define it. The Administrative Quarterly in a study on the subject summarized it this way:

"As we survey the path leadership theory has taken, we spot the wreckage of 'trait theory,' the 'great man' theory, and the 'situationist' critique, leadership styles, functional leadership, and finally, leaderless leadership, to say nothing of bureaucratic leadership, charismatic leadership, group-centered leadership, reality-centered leadership, leadership by objective, and so on."

This summary gives you an idea of the many theories and concepts that have evolved in the attempt to capture the complex nature of this seemingly illusive phenomenon of leadership. However, there are some general principles that are common to all definitions that are worth our consideration.

There is a difference between "leadership" and the "the leader." The leader is the designated position and the individual assuming the position, accepting the responsibility and accountability that accompany the designated position.

Leadership, on the other hand, is the function of the designated position and the exercise of the responsibilities involved in the position. There are many instances where individuals who are designated and placed in position as leaders fail to function and provide leadership. In essence, *a title and position do not guarantee performance and productivity.* Therefore, it is necessary that we understand the differences between the two ideas and have a working definition of both.

LEADERSHIP

A simple and general definition of leadership includes the capacity to *influence, inspire, rally, direct, encourage, motivate, induce, move, mobilize, and activate* others to pursue a common goal or purpose while maintaining *commitment, momentum, confidence,* and *courage.*

Leadership is the organizing and coordinating of resources, energies and relationships in a productive context for an intended result. In its simplest form, leadership is the managing of managers toward a common goal. Therefore, leadership by its very nature incorporates a clear purpose and vision which provide the fuel for inspiration, motivation and mobilization.

Leadership is impossible without a guiding vision and a purpose that generates passion for accomplishment. The vision or guiding purpose is the source from which leadership derives its magnetic field to activate the commitment, corporation and confidence of others. Leadership derives its power from values, deep convictions and correct principles. Leadership is the highest prospect of management.

If you desire to be an effective leader, your principle question would be, "Do I have a guiding vision and purpose that justifies my efforts?" An old proverb says, "He who does not know where he's going will probably end up some place else." King Solomon declares in the book of proverbs, "Where there is no revelation (vision), the people cast off restraint." (Proverbs 29:18). Leadership consists basically of two components: The first is vision and values; the second is inspiring and motivating others to work together with a common purpose. Both components must be in balance if you are to experience effective leadership.

An important ingredient of the leadership function is the ability to draw the best out of other people and inspire them to maximize their potential and that of the resources they manage. *The purest form of leadership is influence through inspiration.* In fact, the greatest and most important aspect of leadership is inspiration.

Inspiration is the opposite of intimidation and is absent of manipulation. There are many so-called leadership situations where fear is the motivator rather than a commitment based on a response to an inspired life. If true leadership gets its source from inspiration, then what is inspiration? Where does it come from? How do you get it? These questions will be dealt with in a later chapter. Now that we know what the leadership function is, let us look at what a leader is.

The discovery of self is the birth of leadership.

PRINCIPLES

1. A title and position do not guarantee performance and productivity.

2. Real qualities of leadership are to be found in those who are willing to suffer for the sake of objectives great enough to demand their whole hearted obedience.

3. Leadership is the organizing and coordinating of resources, energies and relationships in a productive context for an intended result.

4. Leadership is impossible without a guiding vision and a purpose that generates passion for accomplishment.

5. An important ingredient of the leadership function is the ability to draw the best out of other people and inspire them to maximize their potential and that of the resources they manage.

6. The purest form of leadership is influence through inspiration.

NOTES

3

WHAT IS
A LEADER?

"Good Leaders employ others, great leaders deploy themselves and others."

Everyone has the capacity, potential and raw material to become a leader by the design of the creator. However, it is a tragedy that most of the people on this planet will bury the leader trapped within them in the grave of a follower. In fact, many people die without ever knowing who they really were. This is because most of us are mere products of our environment, lacking the will to change, to develop and maximize our potential and become who we really are. How do you become the leader you were born to be? How do you know when you have become a leader?

As I stated before, becoming a leader isn't easy, but learning to lead is a lot easier than you think it is, because God created you with the capacity to lead. You were **born to lead** but you must **become** a leader, just as one may be born a male but must become a man.

Leaders today appear to be an endangered species and in many cases they are being replaced with managers rather than leaders. Others have mistaken being a leader with being a boss. However, it is difficult and perhaps impossible to become something you do not know or cannot define.

Therefore, in this chapter we are going to look at what a leader is, how you can begin your journey to becoming an effective leader and how to refine and further enhance your leadership capacity.

NOT AN ACT OF MAN

The word "leader" is defined as one who guides by influence, or one who directs, by going before or along with. Regardless of title, you cannot be a leader without followers. In essence, a person who has subordinates but no followers, is not a leader. Subordinates who are not followers may be viewed as a resource to be managed, rather than followers to be led. *Simply put, a leader is one who leads others to leadership.* He leads himself first and by so doing, inspires others to follow him into leadership.

A leader is one who influences others to follow after him to a common cause or purpose, and possesses the character which inspires their confidence. At the same time, he is a confident servant. Ultimately, a leader is one who becomes himself fully and attempts to express that self totally.

WHAT MAKES A LEADER

Leaders are not born, but made. Everyone has the capacity and potential to become a leader. But what makes one a leader, and are there distinct characteristics that are common to leadership? A careful study of the lives of effective leaders will reveal some basic ingredients that they all share. They include:

1. PURPOSE

The foundational key to becoming a leader is the discovering and capturing of a sense of purpose for your life. Purpose is the original intent, a reason for the creation or existence of a thing. Discovering personal purpose for your life, is finding reason and meaning for living.

The leader has a clear guiding vision that engenders persistence and perseverance, even in the face of setbacks and failures. He possesses a strong sense of destiny and significance with a deep love for life. In scripture, Jesus Christ and Paul had this ingredient and it served as a guiding force in their every action. Jesus stated, "For this cause/purpose came I into the world." The apostle Paul declared in Philippians 3:13, "But this one thing I do."

2. PASSION

A deep controlling desire that makes the leader's commitment to the guiding purpose a love affair with destiny. The leader loves what he does and loves doing it. His work is his life. Jesus expressed this when he stated, "My food is to do the will of my father."

You must have a deep guiding purpose, a clear vision for your life and a sense of significance. Life without purpose is a study in chaos and an exercise in frustration. Purpose provides the fuel for perseverance, persistence and passion.

3. INTEGRITY

This involves self-knowledge, candor, and maturity. "Know thy self," is the inscription over the oracle of Delphi, and it is still the most difficult task any of us face. But until you truly know yourself, strengths and weaknesses, what you want to do and why you want to do it, you cannot experience any significant success in life. The leader never lies to himself, especially about himself. He knows his flaws and his assets, and deals with them directly. A leader is his own raw material. *The leader strives to discover his full potential.* The leader is one who knows who he is, and accepts himself as worthy and valuable.

Candor is the key to self-knowledge. Candor is based on honesty of thought and action, a steadfast devotion to principle, and fundamental soundness and wholeness. In essence, every leader has a strong spiritual commitment in life. Maturity is also important because every leader needs to have experience and growth through following. He needs to learn to be dedicated, observant and capable of working with others. As a result, he can encourage these qualities in his followers. This ingredient of integrity is one key to becoming a leader.

4. TRUST

Integrity is the basis of trust which is a product of leadership. It is the one quality that cannot be acquired; it must be earned. It is given by co-workers and followers and without it, the leader cannot function. "Trust is a product of time and integrity."

Leaders are individuals whose characters have been tested, proven and established as being faithful and trustworthy. Trustworthiness is a product of character and competence, that is who you are and what you can do. Trustworthiness is the foundation of trust. To become an effective leader you must earn the trust and confidence of others.

5. CURIOSITY AND DARING

To a leader, life is an adventure. Leaders are willing to challenge traditions, experiment with new ideas and explore. A leader is willing to take risks, step out in faith, try new things and challenge convention. He does not worry about failure, knowing he will learn from it.

It is important to note that none of the above ingredients are traits you were born with and cannot change. What is true for leaders is true for all of us; we are our own raw material. Only when we know what we're made of and what we want to be, can we begin to live effectively even in spite of the challenges against us. Leaders are truly like courageous explorers. They have such a strong sense of purpose and security that they welcome the unknown.

It is vital for people to develop their own sense of themselves and their role in the world, and it is equally vital for them to try new things, to test themselves and their beliefs and principles. The world longs for people who will stand up for what they believe, even if they have to stand alone, because we have confidence in such people. *The essence of becoming a leader is knowing and becoming yourself.*

A leader is one who has his or her own value system and beliefs, not someone else's. Most people live their lives walking around in borrowed postures, spouting secondhand ideas, trying desperately to fit in rather than to stand out. True leaders are inwardly directed, self-assured, and as a result truly charismatic. To become a leader, you must know and become yourself. Knowing yourself means separating who you are and who you want to be from what the world thinks you are and wants you to be. No one can teach you how to become yourself and to fully express yourself except you.

To become the leader you were born to be, you must discover who you are, your purpose in life and understand God's design for your existence. Nothing is truly yours until you understand it; not even yourself. When you understand, then you know what to do.

True leaders learn from others, but they are not made by nor become others.

This is the distinctive mark of leaders. Therefore, the ingredients of leadership cannot be taught, they must be learned, and the capacity to learn resides within you.

In essence, no true leader sets out to become a leader. They are simply people who live their lives and express themselves fully. When that expression is one of value, they become leaders. So the point is not to become a leader. The point is to become yourself, to use yourself completely and to use and maximize all your skills, gifts, energies and anointing in order to make your vision and purpose in life a reality.

Leaders are more concerned with expressing themselves, not with proving themselves. It is this full expression that brings glory to God. It is in this light that everyone can become a leader and it is important that you strive to discover who you are and God's purpose for your life.

An Irish proverb says, "You've got to do your own growing, no matter how tall your grandfather is." God created you separate, unique, special, and original. Discover and be yourself and become a leader.

LEADERS, NOT MANAGERS

In any discussion on the subject of leadership and any attempt to define it, it would be essential that we also distinguish the difference between a "manager" and a "leader." It is important that these concepts are understood because there are many situations where managers have been mistaken for leaders and placed in positions in which they are unable to function and perform, thus frustrating the organization and its' objectives.

This difference can be expressed in the saying, "There are four types of people in the world; those who watch things happen, those who let things happen, those who ask what happened, and those who make things happen." Leaders are those who make things happen. Managers are in the other groups. Leaders are those who master the context, managers are those who surrender to it. *All leaders were managers on their way to leadership.* It is the natural path of progression. However, not all managers become leaders.

Jesus speaks of this difference in responsibility in his discourse on the role of a manager in Luke sixteen. He tells the story of a manager who failed to fulfill his responsibility and was unable to account for his time and resources. In this parable, Jesus states a principle that stresses the conditions of transition from manager to leader. Luke 16:10 and 12 states that, "Whoever can be trusted with very little can also be trusted with much, and whoever is dishonest with very little will also be dishonest with much. And if you have not been trustworthy with someone else's property, who will give you property of your own?"

Warren Bennis, professor of Business Administration at the University of California, in his book on leadership recorded some of these differences, and they are enormous and crucial. Study the list below and check your leadership state:

- The manager administers, the leader innovates.
- The manager is a copy, the leader is an original.
- The manager maintains, the leader develops.
- The manager focuses on systems and structure, the leader focuses on people.
- The manager relies on control, the leader inspires trust.
- The manager has a short range view, the leader has a long range perspective.

- The manager asks how and when, the leader ask what and why.
- The manager has his eyes on the bottom line, the leader has his eyes on the horizon.
- The manager imitates, the leader originates.
- The manager accepts the status quo, the leader challenges it.
- The manager is the classical good soldier, the leader is his own person.
- The manager does things right, the leader does the right thing.

Leaders are individuals who have declared independence from the expectations of others and have determined to be true to themselves in the face of a society who wants to homogenize them. If you are to become the leader God intended you to be, then it is necessary to challenge the opinion of others and defy the social straight-jacket that stifles the untapped leader within.

Leaders are individuals who have declared independence from the expectations of others

---

Remember, leadership depends on the ability to make people want to follow voluntarily. They are not made by corporate courses, any more than they are made by college courses, but they are made by experience. A true leader is one who discovers himself, his purpose for living and commits to exploring and expressing himself fully to the glory of God. Simply put, *a leader is one who deploys himself and by so doing, inspires others to do the same.*

Therefore, a true leader is more concerned with deployment rather than employment. He does not attempt to clone people or make everyone else over in his image. His deep desire is to help them discover themselves and deploy their abilities, talents, gifts and potential. To him, as long as people have the same goals, it is not important that they have the same personality. The basic function of the leader is to provide an environment that fosters mutual respect and builds a complementary, cohesive team, where each unique strength is made productive and each weakness is made irrelevant.

True leaders do not try to be; they just are.

PRINCIPLES

1.   Regardless of title, you cannot be a leader
        without followers.

2.   True greatness and true leadership are not
        achieved by reducing men to one's service,
        but in giving oneself in service to them.

3.   A leader is his own raw material.

4.   True leaders are inwardly directed, self-
        assured and as a result, truly charismatic.

5.   The ingredients of leadership cannot be
        taught, they must be learned, and the
        capacity to learn resides within you.

6.   All leaders were managers on their way to
        leadership; however, not all managers be
        come leaders.

7.   Leaders are individuals who have declared
        independence from the expectations of
        others and have determined to be true to
        themselves in the face of a society who
        wants to homogenize them.

WHAT MAKES A LEADER

A. PURPOSE

B. PASSION

C. INTEGRITY

D. TRUST

E. CURIOSITY AND DARING

NOTES

4

THE PURPOSE
FOR LEADERSHIP

"Effective Leadership Makes Itself Increasingly Unnecessary."

E veryone, from their own perspective, desires to be successful. Success could be defined as the effective and efficient completion of an assigned task to the level of expectation of the one who gave the assignment. Success is the fulfillment of the original intent or purpose established by the initiator and source of the assignment.

Therefore, **true success is the fulfillment of original purpose.** Success is not measured by what you have done compared to what others have done, but rather, what you have done compared to what you should have done. Consequently, **the true essence of effectiveness is successful completion of the correct assignment. Effectiveness is not doing things right, but doing the right thing.**

To illustrate, if I invited you to my home for a short stay, and during the course of your stay, I requested that you wash the dishes while I was out on an errand. After my departure you proceeded to the kitchen and began to mop the floor. With great zeal, intensity and energy you scrubbed, mopped, waxed and shined the floor until it was immaculately, flawlessly clean. Pleased with your accomplishment and satisfied with your effort, you smiled at your reflection in the floor with great personal pride.

On my return I entered the kitchen and was deeply impressed and surprised at the excellent condition of the kitchen floor. I had never seen it in such a clean state since I first built the house. Then turning my gaze from the floor, I was shocked to see the dishes undone and still in the same condition I had left them. The result of this episode teaches a principle; you had done a "good" thing but not the "right" thing.

It is possible to zealously, efficiently, successfully and sincerely do an excellent job on the wrong thing and therefore, fail. In the story related above, my house guest failed and was not effective. Even though he did a good thing, he did not do the right thing. He was busy but not effective, active but not progressive. This "right thing" is purpose. *Purpose is the original intent or predetermined result for an individual. It is the expected end.*

It is, therefore, essential and imperative that you know and understand the "purpose" for something before assuming responsibility in a task. Where purpose is not known, abuse is inevitable and precious time, energy and resources are wasted. Effectiveness is not doing a thing right, but doing the right thing. Therefore, in any discussion of effective leadership, it is necessary and essential that we consider the primary purpose for leadership, for in its purpose lies its' effectiveness and success.

Leadership, as conventionally understood, is viewed as the ability of one person to influence others. This fact is supported by the definitions generally given by experts in the field. However, all definitions are the perception of individuals and a product of their cultural experiences. Thus, the only true source of definition for anything is the original purpose for it's existence. To understand the purpose for leadership we must then discover how followers were created and the objective of following, which is the goal of leadership.

THE FOUNDING OF FOLLOWERS

As we noted in the previous chapter, God created mankind and he clearly established his purpose for him when he declared, "Let them rule over all the earth" (Gen. 1:26). This command designated both male and female as God's agents to rule, govern, control and manage God's creation. He declared their leadership ability and responsibility. It is essential that we understand God's principle of potential. God's command for man to rule the planet as his primary purpose, forever established the fact that God has placed within man the capacity and potential to fulfill this command.

Whatever God calls for, He provides for. The assignment is evidence that the ability and potential are within all of us to lead. As I stated earlier, you were created to lead. *You possess the capacity to be a leader within the sphere of your purpose for which you were born.* God did not create followers, but all leaders. So where did followers come from?

The disobedience of man to his Creator's laws and the violation of His principles resulted in man's loss of his position, and that which he was created to rule over began to dominate him. He became a slave to his environment and lost his leadership function. He was unable to fulfill his original purpose. The leader of creation became a follower of it's nature and a victim of it's substances. However, God established a restoration plan to recover man's position, and to train him once again for the position of leader. It is therefore important to consider the following when exploring the purpose for leadership:

THE PURPOSE FOR LEADERSHIP IS NOT FOLLOWERS

The maintenance of followers or subordinates is not the goal of leadership. Many in leadership positions today believe that their leadership should be measured by how many people look to or depend on them. They boast in the fact that they are in great demand by their followers, and actually consider this evidence of their effectiveness. Usually, quite the opposite is true.

These leaders use the dependency factor of their followers to prop up their insecurity and feed their egos. They feed on the needs of others and therefore implement programs and systems that maintain this dependency. This is not the purpose of true leadership. True leadership leads followers into discovering themselves and inspires them to become themselves. The ultimate goal of leadership is independence.

This principle is seen throughout all creation and is established as the key to the essence of life. God created everything to experience three phases.

A) Dependence: every living thing begins life dependent on its source, the fruit on the tree, the fish in the sea, the lion cubs and the birds in the nest and every embryo that clings to the womb.

The second phase is **B) independence:** every living thing must mature to a stage where it detaches itself and expresses it's own individuality and identity. The fruit falls from the tree, the fish finds its own food, the bird learns to fly, and the child eventually becomes independent of his parents.

The third and final stage is **C) interdependence:** after independence, every living thing is responsible for contributing to the ongoing development and replenishing of its species. It produces the seeds of reproduction which the entire species rely on to continue. You can only be truly interdependent after you have become independent. When you have discovered yourself and your unique purpose and identity, only then can you fully contribute to the lives of others. The true nature of leadership is to lead dependents into independence and inspire them to interdependence.

THE PURPOSE FOR LEADERSHIP IS TO PRODUCE LEADERS

The ultimate goal of true leadership is not followers but leaders. *The purpose for leadership is to inspire every follower to become a leader and fulfill his potential.* The true leader measures his success and effectiveness by the diminishing degree of the dependency of his followers. The less they need him; the more effective he is. This principle is seen throughout the scriptures and continually manifests itself in God's encounter with mankind. God has placed within everyone the capacity to be a leader within the context of their purpose in life. The writer of the book of Hebrews states it this way:

In fact, though by this time you ought to be teachers, you need someone to teach you the elementary truths of Gods's word all over again. (Hebrews 5:12).

Jesus expressed this anticipation for the transition from follower to responsible leader on many occasions in words like, "How long shall I stay with you? How long shall I put up with you?" (Matthew 17:17) These words indicate that his purpose for being with them was to eventually leave them to be responsible for the leadership role. In fact, *the ultimate measure of Jesus' success as a leader was the fact that he left.* He saw effective leadership as the ability to release the potential of others and to inspire them to fulfill that potential.

In John 20:21, he declared to his followers, "As the Father has sent me, I am sending you." In Matthew 28:18-19, he further states: "**All authority** on heaven and earth has been given to me. **Therefore go** and make disciples of all nations." Jesus obviously saw authority not as permission to lord over others or to wield power in the affairs of men, but as a vehicle to allow others the freedom to develop and reach their full potential. He employed the disciples so he could deploy their leadership ability.

The true leader measures his success and effectiveness by the diminishing degree of the dependency of his followers.

True leadership brings followers into leadership and makes itself increasingly unnecessary. True leadership is more concerned with being and expressing itself fully, rather than proving itself to others. It's joy is to see others stand in their own integrity and strength, maximizing their potential in God and fulfilling the capacity of their leadership ability. This is the purpose for leadership.

The greatest measure of leadership effectiveness is the level of productivity in your church, business, classroom, government or department in your absence. If your presence is required for followers to function, then your leadership is weak and perhaps ineffective. Remember, the purpose for leadership is to inspire others to exercise their leadership capacity. **You are a successful leader when your followers can lead others.**

Jesus, demonstrated his effectiveness as a leader by leaving. He was so confident of his leadership success, that he transferred the completion of his mission to the leadership of the men he had once called to follow him

The assignment given by the Lord to the leadership of the Church, as presented in the epistle to the Ephesians, clearly signifies the principle of leadership production and reproduction:

He gave some to be apostles, some prophets, some evangelists, some pastors and teachers, to prepare (train) God's people for the works of service (leadership), so that the body of Christ may be built up until we all reach unity in the faith and in the knowledge of the son of God and become mature (responsible, independent), attaining to the whole measure of the fullness of Christ. Then we will no longer be infants.... (Ephesians 4:10-14)

These words confirm God's purpose for setting up leadership in the church to train, develop and produce effective, quality leaders who were transformed from infants into adults, followers into leaders, and dependents to independence. The ultimate test of leadership effectiveness is not how many people are following you, but how many are following them. Simply put, success without a successor is failure.

"To be yourself and become your potential is the essence of life."

PRINCIPLES

1. Everyone has the capacity to become a leader.

2. The purpose for leadership is not the maintenance of followers, but the production of leaders.

4. True leadership inspires others to discover, develop and become themselves.

5. True leadership provides opportunity for others to find and fulfill their God-given purpose.

6. True leaders set others free to become leaders.

7. Success without a successor is failure.

5

ARE YOU LEADERSHIP MATERIAL

*"The greatest display of
leadership is service."*

Qualified leaders are always in demand. Leadership that is authoritative, sacrificial, effective, competent and spiritual. As I stated earlier, simply holding a position of importance does not constitute leadership. Taking a consensus or vote does not make a leader. Resolve does not make you a leader. You could take all the courses you want on how to be a leader and you might still be a follower. **Leadership is born out of character and a determination to be and express yourself fully.** Leadership is the discovery and marriage of purpose, personality and potential.

You must assess your personal motivation for leadership. Are you willing to serve? Are you willing to be patient? Are you willing to say, "I'm available?" You may be available, but are you prepared for the cost and price of leadership? Nevertheless, some people come into leadership with tremendous zeal and little understanding of the dynamics involved. They want to make a difference in this world, but they are not ready for the cost. You are not always prepared to handle full leadership responsibility all at once. Your preparation includes a building of experience. Remember, you can only lead others as far as you've gone yourself.

I believe everyone would like to be a leader. Why? No one wants to be a follower; no one wants to be led around. However, many of us do not understand the dynamics of leadership development and do not know how to take advantage of opportunities to become leaders, while others do not realize their potential as leaders.

Leadership is born out of character and a determination to be and express your self fully.

We will learn many things about the criteria necessary for those who are aspiring and moving toward leadership. Whoever you are and wherever you're at, you can be a leader. Men and women can be leaders in their homes. Young people can be leaders of their friends. Businessmen, lawyers, doctors and nurses can be leaders in their work place.

I want to re-emphasize that a leader is simply a person who has a sphere of influence. However, the degree of that influence and the demands it makes on your potential, determines the magnitude of one's leadership. The janitor is just as important as the CEO. If he doesn't do his job well, you have an uncomfortable atmosphere that will affect the entire organization. If you are given any responsibility, no matter how small, then you are a leader and there are certain qualifications you must meet.

A leader is simply a person who has a sphere of influence.

MOTIVATION AND AMBITION

Some have a great longing to be in leadership, others only a small desire. Regardless of the occupation, the desire to feel like you are master of your situation and in control of your environment resides in each of us. *There is a hidden leader in all of us crying out to be free.* Many of us have this same desire. Even if you're not exactly sure where the desire has come from, I'm informing you, that desire is good. If you are going to be an effective leader, you must be prepared. You have no option.

As we approach the study of some of the basic qualities and characteristics of leadership development, it is essential that we first cover the foundational principle of the underlying motivation for leadership. It is from this motivation that all leadership gets it's essence and context.

The apostle Paul, one of the greatest leaders in history wrote a young man named Timothy concerning leadership and expressed it this way:

If anyone sets his heart on being an overseer, he desires a noble task. (1 Timothy 3:1).

In this verse, Paul clearly states that an ambition for leadership is a good thing. There might be those of you who have a hard time with that because you were raised to believe that the man should be sought, not the other way around.

There are ambitions that do need to be guarded against, like those that are motivated by greed or lust for power. On the other hand, ambition motivated by a desire to serve for example, is an honorable one. A desire to be great is not necessarily sinful. What makes it so is the motivation of the heart.

HEART CONDITION

There seems to be a deep desire in the unregenerate spirit man that dominates and lords it over others. History is full of case studies of people who rose to powerful, leadership positions through both legitimate and illegitimate means. Then, after securing their position, began to expose the true motive of the heart, resulting in the suffering, abuse and destruction of many innocent lives. In every area of life, civic, political, governmental, or spiritual, there are people who aspire to positions of leadership and influence motivated by selfish ambitions.

However, the principle of true leadership is not "self-serving" but "selfless service." A few thousand years ago, the prophet Jeremiah counseled his friend, Barach with these words, "Should you then seek great things for yourself? Seek them not" (Jeremiah 45:5). It should be noted that a desire to be great is not wrong in itself; however, this wise counsel is warning against greatness for "thyself." In short, selfish ambition.

If you want to become a leader so you can be famous, respected, renowned, powerful, important or exercise rulership and authority over others, this is selfish ambition and will end in self-destruction. It violates the principle of respect for the value and worth of all men.

It is essential that we embrace Paul's admonition to "desire leadership," but not for ourselves. Ambition in itself is not sinful or negative. As a matter of fact, the source of the desire to aspire is a product of the nature of God in our created being. Ambition correctly channeled, promotes the nature of God and the welfare of others. In essence, the true leader will never canvass to promote himself.

The fundamental principle of true leadership must begin here, in the heart, for "For out of the overflow of the heart the mouth speaks" (Matthew 12:34). The danger of misguided, unchecked ambition manifested itself in a classic case over two thousand years ago during an exchange between Jesus and his disciples recorded in Mark 10:35-37. James and John requested, "Let one of us sit at your right and the other at your left in your glory." They coveted a position of leadership and power for themselves, not to serve others. At this irresponsible and insensitive request, the Great Leader of leaders used the occasion to teach one of the greatest lessons in motivation and attitude of leadership. He said, "Can you drink the cup I drink?" (verse 38). Here he was establishing the principle that true effective leadership demands personal sacrifice for the sake of others.

"One is not qualified to give orders until he can receive them."

PRINCIPLES

1. Leadership is born out of character and a determination.

2. If you are going to be an effective leader, you must be prepared.

3. Ambition that strives to serve others is honor able.

4. You should be motivated by your love for people, not by your desire to be great.

6

THE PRINCIPLE KEY TO TRUE LEADERSHIP

*"Authority does not make you a leader;
it gives you the opportunity to be one."*

Much of what we call leadership is not true leadership, but a flaunting of authoritarian power. All leaders who do this may have plenty of subordinates but very few followers, without whom he cannot become a leader. This lack of followers is due to three highly predictable responses to the use of power.

1. RESISTANCE: (Fight)

When someone is pushed by someone else; the natural reaction is almost always to push back.

2. RESIGNATION: (Flight)

Most of us do not enjoy fighting, and certainly not a steady diet of it. When faced with a relationship characterized by continual conflict, we try to get away from it. People may tolerate an unpleasant environment temporarily while hoping that it will change. But as that hope wanes, those who find more promising environments tend to leave.

3. SUBMISSION: (Succumb to pressure)

Of the three alternatives, the saddest and most depressing is this one. In some cases, subordinates become almost subhuman. In an attempt to avoid conflict and risk, submissive subordinates make little or no effort to think or contribute to the organization.

This kind of leadership leaves much to be desired. Some lead out of fear, intimidation, obligation, dependency and guilt. But the problem with this type of leadership is that you're creating obedience with a residue of resentment. Ultimately a leader's ability to galvanize his co-workers resides both in his understanding of himself, and in his understanding of his co-workers' needs and wants, along with the mission.

As Peter Drucker has pointed out, "The chief object of leadership is the creation of a human community held together by the work bound for a common purpose." Organizations and their leaders inevitably deal with the nature of man, which is why values, commitments, convictions, even passions are basic elements in any organization. Therefore, an essential for true, effective leadership is that you cannot force people to do very much. They have to be willing to follow. The true leader knows and understands that no human being is going to do what they say. They understand that the only power they truly have as leaders is the power of inspiration.

Inspiration is the key to true leadership. The quality of inspiration is the capacity to cause others to internalize a quality decision, to discover themselves, their purpose and abilities, and to maximize their potential.

To inspire means to activate, stimulate, energize, illuminate, to motivate by divine influence or to breathe into. The word is used in scripture by the apostle Paul in his attempt to explain the source of all scripture:

All scripture is God-breath (inspired) and is useful for teaching, rebuking, correction, and training in righteousness. (2 Timothy 3:16)

In essence, the source of true inspiration is God Himself, and He is the only source of true, effective leadership. Therefore, in order for you to be an effective leader, you must have a personal relationship with God through Jesus Christ, and allow him to breathe into your being a guiding purpose and vision for your life that will strengthen your faith and activate a passion in your heart to accomplish his dream. It is this soul inspired vision, this guiding purpose and passionate drive to fulfill a call, which transforms one from a follower into a leader. For a true leader, his work is not a job or career, but his very life. He lives to fully express and be himself.

It is also this deep commitment to be and express himself that becomes the source of inspiration that stimulates others around the leader to strive to discover and become the best they can be. Inspiration is the essence of true leadership and is the only foundation for willful obedience based on love. Jesus expressed this principle in his appeal to his disciples saying,

If you love me you will obey what I command. (John 14:15)

The implication is that the commitment to help others become the best they can be is the source of inspiration that generates commitment, cooperation and obedience. *Inspiration is the heart of true leadership, and the breath of the Spirit of God is the source of inspiration.* We are leaders to the extent we can inspire others to follow us.

When you discover who you are, why you were born, your true potential and how much you're worth, then and only then can you capture the power of purpose, which generates a passion and thirst for living. When you discover yourself, you become free from the opinions of men and you are motivated by your guiding vision. When you know who you are, what you want and how to go about getting it with correct principles and values, then you will inspire others to join you.

There is only one method of discovering your self-worth, value and purpose, you must return to the manufacturer for his original plan for your life. Become yourself and become a leader.

NATURAL AND SPIRITUAL CHARACTERISTICS OF LEADERSHIP

Leadership that is ordained of God usually comes unsought. In other words, in God's Kingdom, leadership doesn't come to one who is looking for it, someone trying to be the big shot, or who is doing everything to be seen. No, it's the person who is faithful that is ushered into leadership. Faithfulness in the little things is the qualification for promotion to bigger things.

While personality is a prime factor in natural leadership, the true leader influences others not by the power of his own personality alone but by the inspiration of the Holy Spirit. True spiritual leadership can never be self-generated. It is a general principle that we can influence and lead others only as far as we have gone ourselves. The person most likely to be successful is the one who leads not by merely pointing the way, but by having trodden it himself.

In addition to the fact that one must receive inspiration from the Spirit of God to discover the purpose and vision for life, it is also essential to understand that you were created with natural and inherent gifts, abilities, and talents that enhance your leadership effectiveness.

Some of these can be further developed and refined, while others are natural results of your relationship with your Creator. As we endeavor to discover our leadership potential and activate our capacity for effective supervision, it is vital that we look at the differences between the natural and spiritual leadership characteristics.

As noted previously, true leadership does not come as a result of an ambition to lead or be great, but a deep desire to serve others. ***True leadership is not something you grasp but something you become.*** According to the scriptural record, God created all men to dominate (Rule, govern, and control) the earth. As is the nature of all creators or manufacturers, He designed the product with the inherent components, ability and potential to fulfill it's purpose.

Therefore, every product is built with unique elements to fulfill it's purpose, and since man was created for the purpose of leadership, each one possesses natural qualities that are designed to enhance this function.

However, just as the quality of performance and proper maintenance of a product can only be guaranteed by it's manufacturer, even so, these natural leadership qualities and characteristics can only experience their highest effectiveness when they are submitted to and employed by the purposes of God.

Therefore, ***genuine leadership is a marriage of the natural and spiritual qualities producing a well integrated character.*** When these natural,

God-given qualities are exercised in leadership without being submitted to spiritual authority, then abuse and self destruction results. There are countless examples of potentially great leaders who developed and displayed an exceptional degree of natural leadership qualities, but because they neglected the complementary, protective advantage of spiritual qualities, they failed to fulfill their leadership function effectively.

Natural and spiritual leadership can never be self-generated but only be experienced as a result of a personal relationship with the manufacture, our creator. J. Oswald Sanders in his book, Spirit Leadership, when listing the difference between the two qualities leadership elements stated, "Natural leadership and spiritual leadership have many points of similarity, but there are some respects in which they may be antithetical. This is seen when some of their dominant characteristics are set over or against each other."

NATURAL LEADERSHIP	SPIRITUAL LEADERSHIP
1. Self-confident	Confidence in God
2. Knows men	Also knows God
3. Makes own decisions	Seeks God's will
4. Ambitious	Self-effacing
5. Originates own methods	Follows God's methods
6. Enjoys commanding others	Enjoys serving others
7. Motivated by personal interest	Motivated by love
8. Independent	God-dependent

The above lists indicate the basic differences between an individual who attempts to lead without a relationship with God, and one who leads out of that relationship. It is important to observe that all the characteristics that are embraced by the natural leader come as natural results for the one who has a relationship with God.

Self-confidence is a by-product of our faith in God's faithfulness and ability. Thus we can say like the apostle Paul, "I am persuaded that he who has begun a good work in you shall complete it." Or, "If God be for me then who can be against me?" Moses declared at the challenge of the Red Sea:

Do not be afraid. Stand firm and you will see the deliverance the Lord will bring today. The Egyptians you see today you will never see again. The Lord will fight for you; you need only to be still. (Exodus 14:13-14).

This is confidence based on God's faithfulness.

It is also true that as a man knows God, he also learns and understands the nature of mankind. Jesus expressed this fact in John 2:24, "But Jesus would not entrust himself to them, for he knew all men." The spiritual leader's ability to be decisive is also enhanced by the clarity of God's will and purpose. He makes decisions without wavering. It is also his relationship with God that makes the spiritually alive leader more independent than other leaders. This is because his dependency on God creates a freedom from the opinions and criticisms of men. He stands independent of circumstances and environmental influences because of his dependence on God.

Therefore, true leadership will display all the characteristics of natural leadership as well as spiritual, which sets this leader apart from any other.   I encourage you to find God's purpose for your life and place your faith in him to fulfill it and let the leader inside of you come forth with confidence.

There are many of you who have tremendous potential for leadership, but no one has ever encouraged you to discover and express it. As a matter of fact, many people are told that they are nothing. They eventually believe it and waste the talent they have. There are fantastic opportunities and potential in you that God wants to bring out, if you will allow him.

Inspiration is the key to aspiration.

PRINCIPLES

1. As a leader, you cannot "drive" people, you must "lead" them.

2. Real promotion comes from your growth, preparation and experience.

3. Leaders don't draw attention to themselves.

4. You can only lead someone as far as you've gone yourself.

5. Only God gives spiritual authority.

6. Be faithful over a little and you will rule over much.

7. A leader must live every word he speaks.

8. Leaders must be servants.

7

TAPPING YOUR
LEADERSHIP POTENTIAL
PART 1

*"Great leaders are ordinary people who did
extraordinary things because circumstances
made demands on their potential."*

A leader is, by definition, an innovator. He does
things other people haven't done or won't do. He does
things in advance of other people. He makes old
things new, and he makes new things. He doesn't set
out to do great things or to become a leader, he simply
aspires to live life fully and maximize himself. The
great leaders of history were people just like you. They
were not better, smarter, wiser or more gifted than
you, but they developed a passion for life motivated by
a deep guiding purpose and a sense of destiny.

True leaders have nothing but themselves to work
with. They take the self that God has given them and
tap the vast hidden potential that is buried within.
They rise to the top in spite of their weakness.
Abraham Lincoln was subject to fits of depression, yet
he was one of America's greatest presidents. Gideon
was a coward who rose to become a national hero.

What is true of these leaders is also true of all of us.
We are our own raw material. Only when we know

what we are made of and what we want to make of ourselves, can we begin to live our lives effectively. In this chapter, you will be able to assess your leadership potential and the extent of refinement you may need in order to further develop your skills for effective leadership.

Since qualities of natural leadership are by no means unimportant in true spiritual leadership, there is value in seeking to discover leadership potential both in one's self and in others.

An objective study of the following suggested standards of self-measurement could result in the discovery of such qualities where they exist, as well as weaknesses that could be given attention and developed.

TEST FOR LEADERSHIP POTENTIAL

INDEPENDENT DECISION MAKING

Do you think independently? While using the thoughts of others to the maximum, the leader cannot let others do his thinking or make his decisions for him. *Leaders learn from others, but they are not made by others.* Jesus displayed this quality of independent thinking during an encounter with his very own brothers and family. In John 7:1-6, they attempted to influence him to go to the city and make himself known to the world. Even in the face of his own family he declared, "The right time for me has not come; for you any time is right."

To be an effective leader, you may listen to all, but in the end, be responsible for your own decisions.

GOVERN YOURSELF

Do you retain control of yourself when things go wrong? The leader who loses self-control in trying circumstances forfeits respect and loses influence. He must be calm in crisis and resilient in adversity. True leaders take adversity and turn it into opportunity. Leaders learn by leading and they learn best by leading in the face of obstacles. As weather shapes mountains, so problems make leaders. To be an effective leader, you must not only get the group to follow you, but you must be able to convince them that whatever obstacle stands in the way ahead, you're going to get around it. The highest form of Government is self-government. Are you self-disciplined? Do you impose strict discipline and high standards on yourself? This is the mark of leadership.

ABILITY TO CONTROL ANGER

Do you manage your emotions? When someone says something irritating, do you get mad right away? To me, that's a sign of poor leadership ability. God can't trust you with much, because if you are a leader, you're setting yourself up for criticism. It's the people who are the most visible that get all the criticism. All leaders are the targets of criticism. Why? Because they are head and shoulders above the crowd and are the most elevated. They can easily be seen. The minute you become a leader, remember that you are a target. Therefore, you must be able to control yourself and not allow anger to immobilize your rational capacity.

Proverbs 16:32 says, "Better a patient man than a warrior, a man who controls his temper than one who takes a city." In other words, you could be a valiant warrior and still not be a leader. He says, "But a wise man is one who controls his temper." You must have self-control. One of the Fruits of the Spirit is self-control. (Galatians 5:23) Do you have the fruit of the Spirit? Then you must have self-control.

INDEPENDENT THINKER

In every leader there should be an independent thinker. Good leaders are people who can think on their own. They don't think independently of God, but of other people's opinions. Could you imagine what would have been the outcome if Moses had asked for the recommendation of the people in the face of that situation? A true leader doesn't follow the crowd. God can use someone who will think independently. True leaders do not ignore the opinion or contribution of others, they weigh the value of all input, and then make their own decision.

A good leader does not depend on people's opinions to confirm God's will on his life. If God tells you to do something, be very careful who you discuss it with because you'll get many opinions. A good leader thinks independently and must be a decision maker.

There is a good example of this in Joshua's life. He took the children of Israel into the Promise Land because Moses died before they got there.

But if serving the Lord seems undesirable to you, then choose for yourselves this day whom you will serve. Whether the gods your forefathers served beyond the River, or the gods of the Amorites, in whose land you are living. But as for me and my household, we will serve the Lord. Joshua 24:15.

Now that's what I call a leader! Notice, he didn't deny that other options were available to the Israelites. He didn't deny there were other gods to serve, or that the other nations had things that looked attractive. He simply said, "as for me and my house....." He made a decision. Are you an independent thinker?

Have you ever broken yourself of a bad habit? To lead others, you must master yourself. It takes personal integrity and desire to break a bad habit. It's very difficult to lead others if you cannot master yourself. As a matter of fact, there are a lot of tragedies in church leadership today because we have many leaders who want to master the body of Christ, but are failing to master themselves. The same is true in political, civic and other arenas of leadership endeavors. If you possess the inner strength to break deeply imbedded habits, such as procrastination, criticizing, overeating, or oversleeping, then you have begun to tap the leadership potential within you.

**You cannot fully conquer kingdoms
until you have conquered yourself.
Leaders master themselves.**

Paul says it clearly in the book of Timothy. He says if a man desires the ministry of a bishop or a deacon, he must first master his own house. How can he master the house of God when he cannot master his own house? I would suggest that house is not just the dwelling of your family, but also your physical body as the house of God. You cannot fully conquer kingdoms until you have conquered yourself. Leaders master themselves.

CREATIVELY HANDLE DISAPPOINTMENTS

True leaders see disappointments as opportunities to maximize their potential and they learn from surprise. A good leader has the ability to stay calm in a crisis. When Jesus and his disciples were out in their boat during a storm, Jesus fell asleep. Although the disciples had potential, Jesus established his leadership by keeping control of his emotions.

The apostle Paul also demonstrated how a leader handles disappointments. He, other prisoners and their Roman guards were on a ship headed toward Rome. Suddenly, a storm came up and they began to sink. God was with them however, and they drifted onto an island called Malta. You might think, "What a disappointment." Not Paul, he began preaching and the entire island was saved. The Bible says that the people asked Paul to stay and when he left, there was a church established on the island. Paul made an appointment out of a disappointment.

When Moses reached the Red Sea, the people started crying out because they were afraid. Pharaoh was behind them and the Red Sea was before them. They could hardly believe Moses when he said to them, "Be still. Everything is in order. Stand still and see the salvation of the Lord." Then Moses ran to God and cried out, "Lord, help!" Leaders know how to keep self-control in crisis. That's why they are leaders. Leaders have to be in charge, even when they don't feel like they are. Sometimes your knees may get shaky, but you must stand.

This means that you must be an example of what others should do. They will imitate you. If Moses started crying in front of the people, they would also have cried. I can picture Moses going behind a rock and saying, "Now, what are we going to do, Lord? I've got them all calm. Now you must come through."

The Lord said, "Why are you crying to me? Tell the Israelites to move on." In other words, "I told you all to leave Egypt, but you're going in Egypt's direction." You see, Moses knew he was on the right track, but the circumstances didn't look too good. He knew how to control himself in difficult times. Can you keep yourself calm in crisis? Keep asking yourself, "Am I qualified to be a leader?"

> **A fool gives full vent to his anger, but a wise man keeps himself under control.**
> (Proverbs 29:11)

Leaders maintain peace in adversity, not because they deny its presence, but because of their confidence in their guiding purpose, their deep commitment to the vision and total trust in their Divine source and the potential he has placed within them. True leaders are never limited by natural limitations. They see beyond the restrictions and embrace the impossible. How do you handle disappointment?

INSPIRES CONFIDENCE

Do you readily secure the cooperation and win the respect and confidence of others? Jesus had something very important to say about usability. He said, "He that has much, much is expected. And if the person who has much exercises much, more to him will be given." He's talking about ability and responsibility. Jesus also said, "If you have not been faithful over a little, I can't make you ruler over much." Many people want to go from the crib to the throne, instantly. They want to be the leader, or the president, or the evangelist, right now. Not even Jesus came into His full ministry until He was 30.

A good leader is someone people can have confidence in. Do you readily secure the trust and support of others? If you do, then you are on your way to being a leader. The only way for others to have confidence in you is to see that you are faithful over little things, committed to your purpose and willing to die for your cause.

Many times in our spiritual development, the Lord asks us to do things that we might consider unpleasant at the moment. It might be a short-term mission trip to a third world nation where your personal comfort will be challenged. You might say, "Lord, I think you've made a big mistake." The Lord does that because he's trying to build character in you and work disobedience out of you. He wants to have confidence in you. If you were disobedient in the little things, then imagine what would happen if you were in charge of something big.

Paul took young John Mark on one of his missionary journeys, but he didn't test his confidence and faithfulness. Halfway through, John Mark couldn't handle it anymore and he quit. Paul told him, "Go back home."

Genesis 39:2, "The Lord was with Joseph and he prospered, and he lived in the house of his Egyptian master." Joseph was under Potiphar and when he saw that Joseph was responsible, he put him in charge of his house. When Joseph first arrived in that house, he was just a slave. When he proved himself faithful, he was promoted. Verse 5, "From the time he put him in charge of his household and of all that he owned, the Lord blessed the household."

When people have confidence in your leadership, your work will prosper. You will be surrounded by faithful workers who bring fresh, new ideas and a better way to do things. They don't sit and wait to be told what to do.

RELIABLE

Are you entrusted with handling difficult and delicate situations? True leaders are sought out for advice and assistance in delicate circumstances. Daniel is our example of this quality. He was a great man of God. When you think of Daniel, you think of the lion's den. But that was only a few hours out of Daniel's life. His life is full of so many other events.

In Chapter 6 verse 1 it reads, "It pleased Darius, the king, to appoint 120 satraps to rule throughout the kingdom with three administrators over them." Daniel was one of the three administrators. This man of God was a politician; a Spirit filled politician. If you think that Christians are supposed to be in the background, read this scripture again. God wants us where the action is and Daniel was right there.

Now Daniel was so good at his job that the king put him over the other administrators as well. Of course, this made them jealous and they began to look for corruption in his life.

Verse 4 says, "They could find no corruption in him, because he was trustworthy and neither corrupt nor negligent." Wouldn't it be wonderful to work with someone who wasn't negligent, someone who kept their word? Trustworthiness is an essential leadership quality.

CORRECTION

Do you possess the ability to secure discipline without having to resort to a show of authority? True leadership is an internal quality of spirit that does not require an external show of force. True leaders inspire others to become better and therefore engender a sense of behavioral expectation and trust that becomes a source of self discipline. If others reprimand themselves when they disappoint you, then you are leading by inspiration. Peter, after denying Jesus, demonstrated this quality by self-imposed shame.

MOBILIZATION

Can you induce people to happily do some legitimate thing that they would not normally wish to do?
Is your vision so strong and so God-inspired, that
people begin to help you with it, even though they may
not have wanted to do it initially? Let's consider the
disciples. When Jesus said, "Let's go to Samaria,"
they didn't want to. They said, "We don't mix with the
Samaritans." So Jesus sat on a well, right outside
Samaria to help them see the vision that he had for the
Samaritans. When it was all over, the whole town
invited Jesus in, and all the disciples went along.

I believe most of the Samaritans were looking
around saying, "These Jews are in our town?" And
Peter might have said, "I'm only here because of him."
Of course, after Peter got filled with the Holy Ghost, he
went there by himself and a whole house was converted. The key to mobilizing others is inspiration.
If you can inspire, you can mobilize. This is leadership. Leadership makes full use of human resources,
and identities, develops new talents and releases
human potential.

CONCILIATOR

Are you considered a peace maker, one who finds
it easier to keep the peace than to make peace where
it has been shattered? An important function of
leadership is conciliation; the ability to discover
common ground between opposing viewpoints and
then induce both parties to accept it. This ability
comes from wisdom and wisdom comes from the

word of God. A good leader does not depend only on the knowledge of this world, but he is also filled with the word of God. He judges everything in light of Gods' wisdom.

ANTAGONISM

Leaders possess the quality of openness. Can you accept opposition to your view point or decision without considering it a personal affront and reacting accordingly? Leaders must expect opposition and must not be offended by it. True leaders are able to share ideas, reasons and rationale, while maintaining genuine respect for the ideas of others.

RELATIONSHIPS

True leaders are not afraid to establish strong friendships because they are secure in themselves. Also, it doesn't make sense for you to be a leader if you keep making enemies, they consider all negative behavior toward them as temporary insanity, based on ignorance. You can always tell a leader because someone's following them. Therefore, making friends is important. True leaders have no enemies.

The Bible says that he who keeps his mouth and speaks kind words will find favor with all men. God wants you to have favor. The Bible also says, "And Jesus increased in wisdom and in stature and in favor with God and man" (Luke 2:52). How are you going to win somebody who's mad at you? "The brother offended is harder to win than a city with walls" (Prov. 18:19). The scriptures also state that if we obey God and follow him, he will make even our enemies to be at peace with us (Prov. 16:7). There are many ambitious, young leaders who have the right heart but the wrong head. They have the right message but the wrong method. They keep creating enemies. True leadership speak the truth with love and sensitivity.

They make friends before making converts. They attract people because they express a spirit of acceptance, withholding judgement, giving the benefit of the doubt, and making people aware of their own importance, worth and value. Do people seek your company?

UNCONDITIONAL ACCEPTANCE OF OTHERS

Are you really interested in people, in all people of all types and all races? Or do you entertain respect of persons? Is there hidden racial prejudice? An antisocial person is unlikely to make a good effective leader. True leaders unconditionally accept and cherish the value of others. They see all men as equal and strive to bring out the best in everyone.

There are ministers who may preach to you, but may not like you. They only care as much for you as what you put in the offering. They don't want to know how you're doing through the week; they don't want to check on you or your family. They just want to stand up before you and perform. A leader called by God becomes a people lover. *You cannot really help people if you don't like them.* The Bible says, "The good shepherd gives his life for the sheep."

Let me give you an example of how you can tell whether or not you are an effective, people-loving leader. In John 4:4-42 we find the story of the woman at the well. Jesus had just finished a big crusade and he was tired. He and his disciples began walking toward Samaria.

Verse 5 says, "So he came to a town in Samaria called Sychar, near the plot of ground Jacob had given his son Joseph. Jacob's well was there, and Jesus, tired as he was from the journey, sat down by the well. It was about the sixth hour. When a Samaritan woman came to draw water, Jesus said to her, 'Will you give me a drink?' (His disciples had gone into town to buy food.)

The Samaritan woman said to him, 'You are a Jew and I am a Samaritan woman. How can you ask me for a drink? (For Jews do not associate with Samaritans.)" This woman had prejudice.

It's very difficult to be a representative of God if you are prejudiced. Every man on the face of the earth is made in God's image. The Bible says, "No man can say he loves God if he hates his brother. For how can you say you love God whom you cannot see,

and hate your brother whom you can see." (I John 2)
It's amazing how we aspire to be leaders, yet we don't
realize this very basic principle of just loving people.

Jesus goes on to say, "'If you knew the gift of God
and who it is that asks you for a drink, you would have
asked him and he would have given you living water.'
'Sir,' the woman said, 'you have nothing to draw with
and the well is deep. Where can you get this living
water? Are you greater than our father, Jacob, who
gave us the well and drank from it himself, as did also
his sons and his flocks and herds?" Jesus answered,
'Everyone who drinks this water will be thirsty again,
but whoever drinks the water I give him will never
thirst. Indeed the water I give him will become in him
a spring of water welling up to eternal life.' The woman
said to him, 'Sir, give me this water.' He told her, 'Go
call your husband.' 'I have no husband.'"

Notice that Jesus was not only concerned about
getting her saved, but he wanted to meet her personal
needs as well. Don't be so concerned about getting
people converted that you forget that they have needs
and problems. Jesus said, "Woman, you have a need.
I want to help. Where do you hurt the most?" She was
hurting in her domestic life so Jesus zeroed in on her
problem and asked, "How's your husband?" The
woman said, "I have no husband."

Jesus said to her, "You are right when you say you
have no husband. The fact is, you have had five
husbands, and the man you now have is not your
husband. What you have just said is quite true.'"

When people read this story, this poor woman seems to always get the bad end of the deal. In those days, if a woman was married to a man and couldn't have children, the man could divorce her and leave. She was probably kicked out of one house and another man took her in, married her, and when she didn't have any children kicked her out as well, and so on.

After the fifth husband, can you imagine how she must have felt about men? How do you think she felt about society? Here was a woman who apparently was the topic of gossip for years. After so much frustration she must have finally decided, "I'm just going to live with this one so he won't have the chance to disgrace me by divorcing me." She was rejected, dejected and depressed.

Jesus listened intently as she said, "I can see you're a prophet." Jesus began to tell her, "Believe me woman, a time is coming when you'll worship the Father neither in this mountain nor in Jerusalem. You Samaritans worship what you do not know; we worship what we do know, for salvation is from the Jews. Yet, a time is coming and has now come when the true worshipers will worship the Father in spirit and truth, for they are the kind of worshipers the Father seeks. God is a spirit, and his worshipers must worship in spirit and in truth."

Look at her answer carefully, "The woman said, 'I know that Messiah,' (called Christ,) 'is coming. When he comes, he will explain everything to us.' Jesus said, 'I who speak to you am he.' Just then his disciples arrived and were surprised." Here is where you can begin to tell the difference between a leader and his followers. Followers will usually be surprised when a leader stands up and does something unexpected.

The disciples were surprised to find Jesus talking with a woman. That sounds strange, but in those days, any man who claimed to be a respectable man never spoke to a woman in public. That's where Paul got the idea of women keeping silent in the church, it was a social and cultural problem.

Here was Jesus talking to a woman. The disciples couldn't handle it. He broke tradition. He destroyed their pre-conceived ideas about God. He killed prejudice.

As much as the disciples wanted to, they did not ask Jesus why he was talking to the woman; they were afraid to ask. They knew that every time they asked Jesus a question, he would confound them. They had decided that they were going to keep silent because they didn't want to be embarrassed in front of one another. They knew that if Jesus was talking to a woman then it must be all right, because he'd been right all along.

The second reason they were surprised was that it was not common for Jews to associate with Samaritans. Not only was she a woman but she was a Samaritan woman.

I like verse 28 and 29, "Then leaving her water jar, the woman went back to the town and said to the people, come see a Jew." Was that what she said? No. Come see a Rabbi? No. Let's compare what this woman said with her earlier statement. Verse 9: "You are a Jew." Verse 29: "Come, see a man." She started out prejudiced and ended up human.

A leader treats everybody the same because everyone has needs, problems, and hurts that are the same. What is it that everyone needs? The white man, the Indian, the black man, the Haitian, the Korean, the Chinese, the Japanese, they all need love and respect, just like you and I. *A good leader knows how to love people just as they are.*

SELF-CONFIDENT

Are you intimidated by others and compare yourself with the abilities and accomplishments of others? Are you at ease in the presence of your superiors or strangers? Did God call you? Sure he did. The Bible says that you didn't call Him. God promises that if you follow Him, He will take you before kings. To become a leader, you must possess a deep sense of security, which represents our sense of worth, identity, emotional anchor, self-esteem and personal strength. Self-confidence finds its source in confidence in a Higher Authority.

In Acts 5:29, Peter and the apostles were brought before the Sanhedrin, the ruling religious council of their day. Peter was full of the Holy Ghost and a leader created by God. Jesus had worked with him for three and a half years, until he had become a man of God. Verse 28, "We gave you strict orders not to teach in His name. Yet you have filled Jerusalem with your teaching and are determined to make us guilty of this man's blood?" Peter and the other apostles replied, "We must obey God rather than men! The God of our father raised Jesus from the dead-whom you had killed by hanging him on a tree." He knew that there is only one superior and that's Jesus Christ.

A true leader is never intimidated by anyone because he is confident in himself in Christ, and is aware that nobody is better, just different from him. He knows that all men have the same value before God.

Begin to cultivate the leadership qualities that you have within you. Take your responsibility with confidence, integrity and faithfulness. The more you do so, the more God is going to give you to do.

God cannot use a man who's afraid of other people. How do you behave when you're with your boss? Do you say what you want to? Or, do you say what you think he wants to hear? People who have confidence in God and their own ability have no fear of men.

The Bible says in Proverbs, "The fear of man is a snare" (Prov. 29:25). Snare is the same word we use today for trap. When you're caught in a snare, you can't move. You can't say what you want to and so you never progress in your leadership. Perhaps you haven't been promoted because your boss sees you as a person who has no confidence in yourself. True leaders love confident people.

I think one of the greatest examples of this is Jesus. Here's a man whose hands were bound, whose back was bleeding and whose beard was plucked out. Standing before the great and powerful Pilate, he seemed to be nothing but a mutilated, weak and insignificant man. Pilate said to him, "Do you know who I am?" Jesus had stood before Herod as well and Herod had also said to him, "Do you know I have the power to give you your life or take it?"

Standing before these earthly rulers, Jesus could have been intimidated. Instead, He said, "Pilate, you could have no power over me except it was given to you from my Father. Just to show you that I came for the purpose of dying, you go ahead and condemn me, I'm going to let you do your job." Jesus was a man who knew who he was. *True leaders know who they are,* and the authority under which they function.

APPROACHABLE

Do your subordinates appear at ease in your presence? A true leader has a sympathetic, understanding, friendly and open attitude that will put others at ease. True leaders really care and love everyone with an unconditional attitude and always seeks the potential within others. He never confuses their behavior with their worth.

The attitude of true leaders is cheerful, pleasant, happy, optimistic and upbeat. Their spirit is enthusiastic, hopeful and believing. This attitude and countenance is infectious and contagious like an energy field drawing the best out of others. They believe in other people and always extend a spirit of forgiveness and acceptance.

EGO STRENGTH

Are you unduly dependent on the praise and approval of others? If you are always needing and wanting praise and approval, then you are still a follower and not a leader. Throughout the Bible there are illustrations of people of God who had this problem and every one of them failed.

In Genesis 40, Joseph is called upon to interpret the dreams of Pharaoh's baker and cup-bearer who were in prison with him. To the cup-bearer, Joseph told of a coming promotion and to the baker, he predicted his coming death. God had given the interpretation and Joseph was obligated to give it accurately. If he had been concerned with the approval of others, he might have been tempted to lie or at least shade the truth, but Joseph wanted only God's approval and so he did what was right.

Many times you even have to go against the approval of your own family. If you are tempted to compromise in order to gain the approval of others, don't do it. Have confidence in what you have heard from God.

True leaders do not become controlled by the accolades of others nor their opinions. Throughout the Bible, you'll find the leaders that God raised up going against the grain most of the time. Religious leaders at the time of John the Baptist were wearing linen, silk and satin. Instead of these things, he wore camel's wool. He came out of the wilderness saying, "I've got the word of God." The Pharisee's response was, "You aren't dressed like we are." But their opinions of him did not affect him.

Though they accused him of all kinds of evil and terrible things, John was steadfast in his mission and focused in the face of disapproval. Be willing to stand for the right, and correct principle, committed to your purpose even if you have to stand alone.

CENTERED

Do you possess a strong and steady will? A leader will not retain his position long if he is vacillating. If you want to be an effective leader, you must possess a strong and steady will. Many people have the strong will, but they haven't got the steady will. Steady means consistent, to stick with it. If you want to be used effectively as a leader, you have to be stable and consistent.

In Exodus chapter 32 there is a negative example of this principle. Moses had left the people in the wilderness and had gone up into the mountain to talk with God. He was there for so long that the people became frustrated. They said, "Moses must have died." Aaron was in charge while Moses was away and when he returned verse 21 says, "Moses came and he said to Aaron, 'What did these people do to you, that you led them into such great sin?'"

Notice how Moses asks the question, "What did these people do to you?" Aaron replied, "Do not be angry, my lord, you know how prone these people are to evil." He was blaming the sin on the people even though he had been in charge. Aaron continued, "They said to me, 'Make us gods who will go before us.'"

Aaron's response is an indication of his weak leadership. His phrase, "They said," implies his decisions were influenced, controlled and subjected to the opinions and wishes of the people. He was no longer leading the people, but was being led by the people. This is the fundamental principle of democracy, the philosophy of leadership by the will of the majority.

This form of leadership and governing is at first glance attractive, honorable and seemingly fair. My personal conviction is that this form of leadership is the best system fallen man has developed to safeguard himself against unbridled abuse of his fellow man. Democracy is not a principle of God, but an invention of man. It is man's best attempt to provide a system of governing sinful men.

However, the major flaw of democracy is that its authority flows from the bottom up, rather than from the top down, as it does in the Kingdom of God. Secondly, the very premise of democracy lends itself to the appeasement of the masses, as opposed to commitment to truth and right. In essence, democracy in action may violate principles in order to maintain its existence. Democracy can only be effective if its constitution is based on and committed to correct principles. Simply put, democracy is leadership by the people, not the leader. The leader must be true, otherwise the people will not be committed to his principles, convictions or personal purpose.

No where in the Bible do you find democracy in the leadership of God's church. I know we love democracy, but that was invented by the Greeks, not God. God's kingdom is a theocracy. In other words, what he says goes, even if you don't agree. That's the way God operates. When God calls you to be a leader, he gives you his word and his word stands, no matter who disagrees with him.

This must not be construed to mean that the need for cooperation and participatory management would be ignored. There must be an environment of cooperation and teamwork for there to be corporate success. However, this must be done within the context of a singular vision and guiding purpose.

I appreciate all the leadership ideas and philosophies we have in our nations. In the church strata especially there are many different types of church governments, but when it comes to the ministry of God, there is no democracy. If God said it in his word you do it, no matter who disagrees with you.

Now here is Aaron and instead of leading, he is being led. It is important to understand that you can't lead people when they're leading you. As Aaron continued it got a little worse, "As for this fellow Moses, we don't know what has happened to him. So, I told them, 'Whoever has gold jewelry, take it off.' Then they gave me the gold, and I threw it into the fire, and out came this calf!" Wait a minute, let's be sensible. The calf just came together by itself, walked out of the fire, and said "Worship me?" Come on, that's ridiculous. Aaron probably designed the idol and instructed them on how to build it.

If you are the kind of leader who just lets things happen, you won't be in a leadership position very long. There are three kinds of people in the world. The first person is under the circumstances, the second is a victim of the circumstances, and the third is a person who creates his own circumstance. A leader is the third kind of person.

King Saul was the kind of person who was under the circumstance. There were thousands of Philistines camped on the hills, so many that they looked like ants, all armed with knives, daggers, spears and shields. And there was Goliath, ten feet tall, screaming, cursing, and threatening God's people. Saul felt that all the circumstances were against him. He said, "Whew, that's a big man. We can't kill him." And the Bible says that the Israelites were afraid.

Then David came along bringing his brothers' lunch, and he heard Goliath. David walked up to his brothers and asked, "Who's that guy over there?" Everyone was under the circumstances and they didn't know what to do.

David created his own circumstance. He said, "Who is this uncircumcised Philistine? How dare he defy God! Let me get at him." Imagine, a fourteen-year old boy put the king and all his best soldiers to shame. David walked up to Goliath and said, "I'm going to have your head, today. I'm going to cut it off and feed you to the birds." Goliath laughed, "Who's this little runt that's come here to make me ashamed in front of my people? Go get me a man." David replied, "You're looking at him." He changed the circumstance.

What do you do when everything is against you? Do you act like Saul and say, "Whew, this is a big problem, we're never going to get out of this one, we're going to lose the house." Or, "Everybody has a job except me, there are no jobs left in the city. I'm going to die of starvation." If that is what you think then you're looking at the circumstances. Why don't you create your own? I love to hear somebody say, "Since there are no jobs out there, I'm going to create my own job, 'Mama, can I borrow your lawn mower?'" Create your own circumstances.

When I was at Oral Roberts University, I had a roommate named Steve. When Steve was completing up his last year, he ran out of money. Do you know what he did? Steve, a senior at the University, borrowed a friend's lawn mower. He took that lawn mower and began to mow people's lawns and collect a few dollars. After graduation, I heard from a mutual friend that Steve now has his own company and is making over $100,000.00 a year. When I asked what kind of company he had my friend replied, "A lawn mowing company." He had created his own circumstances. He had a strong and steady will and he didn't let the situation rule him.

7

TAPPING YOUR
LEADERSHIP POTENTIAL
PART 2

FORGIVING

Do you nurse resentments or do you readily forgive injuries done to you? You can never be used effectively in leadership if you nurse resentments. Now to nurse something is like nursing a baby, you keep holding onto it, you don't want it to die. Someone hurts you and 10 years later when you see them again, you still want to get even with them. Don't nurse it. God can not effectively use you if there's unforgiveness in your heart. If you have any unforgiveness, you negate the whole possibility of God using you effectively. True leaders are so secure, they can easily forgive and ask for forgiveness without hesitation.

In Genesis chapter 40 we find the story of Joseph. If anyone could nurse resentment, it should have been Joseph. When Joseph was a young boy, his brothers threw him into a pit, sold him into slavery, and then told his father that he had been killed. He could have carried that in his heart for years, but he didn't because he was a leader.

Verse 46, "Joseph was 30 years old when he entered the service of Pharaoh." When God decides to do something He does it right. When I read this it makes me feel so good. This means that the Lord doesn't have to wait until you're 60 to use you. He'll use you when you're 30, or 16, or 10, he'll use you right now. "And Joseph went out from Pharaoh's presence and traveled throughout all Egypt. Joseph collected all the food and produce for 7 years."

Then in chapter 42 Joseph's brothers came to Egypt. "And so he said to them, go and bring my younger brother and then we'll discuss things." After they had done that, Joseph revealed himself to his brothers and embraced them. He didn't nurse resentment.

We don't have time as leaders to put up with petty, childish resentments. God doesn't have the time to waste on people that babysit resentments. Good leaders never nurse resentments, they learn how to forgive, and they do it easily.

True leaders don't overreact to negative behaviors, criticism or human weakness. They don't feel built up when they discover the weakness of others. They are aware of their own weakness as well. They also realize that behavior and potential are two different things. They believe in the unseen potential of all people. They feel grateful for their blessings and are able to naturally, compassionately forgive the offenses of others. They don't carry grudges. True leaders know their feelings, perceptions and opinions are not facts and therefore, act on that awareness which takes thought control and fosters humility.

PURPOSEFUL

Do you have a driving, guiding vision that grips your soul with passion such as Paul who said; "This one thing I do?" Such a singleness of mind will focus all one's energies and powers on the desired objective.

Have you found a deep, soul-grounded cause or reason to live? Is there a vision in your heart that gives life to your motivation? This is the mark of leadership. Leaders not only have something to live for, but they have found something to die for. ***Until you are willing to die for what you are living for, you cannot become a true leader.***

ENCOURAGING

Are you reasonably optimistic? Pessimism is no asset to a leader. Suppose your boss kept telling you, "We're losing money, we're going down the drain, this company is going to close." What would you begin to think? Would it be, "I'm going to lose my job, I'm going to get fired." A good leader is always optimistic.

I'll give you a good example of this quality. Genesis chapter 39 verse 22, "So the warden put Joseph in charge of all those held in the prison, and he was made responsible for all that was done there." In those days they didn't have nice jails like we do now. At that time, they threw you into a pit, where there was no bathroom, furniture or dining room. That pit was your bathroom, your bed, your dining room and everything else. Joseph was thrown into one of these pits, yet he remained optimistic. He kept a steady will.

Eventually, the Chief Jailer saw in Joseph a man who had self-confidence and elevated him above the others in the prison. While he was in jail he interpreted dreams for people and helped them out. That's optimism. When we reach a position such as this, what do we do? "Oh, Lord, why did you put me here. I've served you all these years and look what you've done. I've been a faithful choir member, I've been faithful to attend church and look what's happened to me. Why did my house burn down? Why did I lose my job?" This attitude does not lend itself to effective leadership development.

Let's start talking the way God talks. He says, "Out of the miry clay I will lift you up and put your feet on a rock to stay." That's what he says in Psalms. He said that many are the afflictions of the righteous, but the Lord will deliver you out of them all. Instead of worrying about the affliction you're in, start thinking about the way God will lift you out. *A good leader remains optimistic.* Your attitude will determine your altitude.

In this ministry we sometimes have pressing needs, but we believe in a God who meets needs, and we don't walk around saying, "How are we going to do this, how are we going to do that?" We know how we're going to do it, through the power of God. Jesus said, "Without me, you can do nothing," and he also declared "nothing is impossible if you believe!

RESPONSIBILITY

Leaders love Responsibility. Do you welcome responsibility? If someone says to you, "I'd like for you to vacuum the rug in the sanctuary." Accept the responsibility as a road to leadership. Think of yourself as the leader over the vacuum cleaner, with responsibility to God. God's watching you to see just how well you perform in this area. But if you're in a hurry, and you only clean the front part (that everybody's going to see), leaving the back part dirty (since no one's going to see that), the Lord will take note. He will say, "You are half-hearted." Now, do you think the Lord is going to give you greater responsibility? This is important because the Bible says, "If you'll be faithful over a little, I'll make you ruler over much."

Responsibility denotes the ability to respond to the situation. Leadership is fostered in the individual who believes that within him lies the potential to face and handle any task. He is not afraid to make decisions and accept the consequences of those decisions. This is the exercise of responsibility.

Some people are afraid of a little responsibility. There are many in the body of Christ who are praying to God that the preacher or their supervisor doesn't ask them to do anything. "Oh Lord, don't let him ask me to be an usher, don't let him ask me to cook any food, don't let him ask me to clean the rugs, Oh God, please don't let him ask me" That's their prayer.

God will use someone who loves responsibility. They are willing and they welcome it all the time. They are asking, "Can I help with anything, can I do anything else?" That's the kind of people I like around me.

I have a friend named Leroy who is a man of God. The Lord uses him to minister to me in ways that nobody knows. Leroy is always asking, "Is there anything else I can do?" There's always something to do, but there are people who will avoid me because they know that. They avoid work, yet when God wants to do something great they're the first ones who want to go along. Imagine the Lord saying , "You know I've been watching you for 12 months, and when the work gets hard, you're the first one to go home. I'll use someone who's willing to work." If you're going to be lazy, be lazy by yourself where nobody else can be influenced by you.

A good leader is somebody who is always excited about responsibility. We've been reading the story about Joseph. All Joseph did was tell Pharaoh the interpretation of a dream. And what did Pharaoh say? "I want you to take charge of my house, of my servants, of the land, of the economics of the country, and of the social work, you are in charge." Did Joseph say, "But I've never been to university to `study social work, I don't know anything about economics, and I don't know anything about politics." No, he said, "When do you want me to start?"

It says in the Bible that he took the chariot and went throughout the city checking out his new responsibility. What do you do when you are given responsibility? Do you say, "They are always picking on me and asking me to do something." There are two reasons why we pick on you: **1)** you're lazy, and we're trying to get you moving or **2)** you're the kind of person who always wants responsibility, you like it and we can use you and depend on you. If you qualify in that last area, you're on your way to leadership.

THE MARK OF A GOOD LEADER

When people fail, a good leader doesn't treat them as failures, he corrects them and tries to help them learn their lessons so they can do it better the next time. He doesn't throw the baby out with the bath water. There are many people who, when you make one mistake, they cancel you. They don't want you around any more, they don't want to talk to you anymore, they put you aside because they don't want to deal with you. To me that's poor leadership. *True leaders are not annoyed by people's failures, they are challenged by them.* They do not consider the behavior, but the potential within. Leaders separate a person's behavior from their self worth and does not confuse their value with them present condition.

In every organization or ministry there will be opportunities to fail, and some people do fail. Leaders need to realize that everybody can fail and instead of making that person feel degraded and unusable, take that person, lift them up and say, "Look, you didn't do it right, so let me show you how to do it."

Some people make mistakes and the first thing they say is, "I'm never going to be worth anything. My mom always told me that I was a failure, my grandma told me that nothing worthy could come out of my life, and the teachers told me that I was a loser." That's what some people do, and they sit down in a puddle of failure and bathe themselves. For years they stay in that puddle.

If you want to be a leader in God's kingdom, you must be a person who knows how to deal effectively with your failures and the failures of others. You can look at failures as lessons, and then you move on. Don't stay in your failures. Good leaders encourage other people to get out of their failure. That's important. Think about Jesus and Peter. How many times did Peter fail Jesus? If you missed your exit on the highway of life, don't continue in the wrong direction. Stop, turn around and get back on track. Remember, *failure is only a temporary detour and should never become a permanent address.*

I want to encourage you to seek usefulness. Whoever seeks leadership, desires a worthy task. There are many who will sit down in their chairs and warm them, hoping that someone will tell them to be a leader. They sit for years, waiting, and they die waiting. We should desire leadership. A better way to phrase this is, to be available. To say, "I want to do something." That's a good attitude to have. Then step out in faith and do it!

As in every seed there is a forest,
so in every follower their is a leader.

PRINCIPLES

1. A leader is an innovator.

2. If you want to be a leader in God's Kingdom, you've got to be a person who knows how to deal effectively with your failures and the failures of others.

3. Leaders learn from others, but they are not made by others.

4. Leaders learn by leading and they learn best by leading in the face of obstacles. As weather shapes mountains, so problems make leaders.

5. When people have confidence in your leadership, your work will prosper.

6. True leaders really care and love everyone with an unconditional attitude and always seeks the potential within others. He never confuses their behavior with their worth.

7. Good leaders do not become controlled by the accolades of others nor their opinions.

TEST FOR LEADERSHIP POTENTIAL

Rate yourself on the following chart and check your leadership potential.

		Yes	No	Sometimes
1.	INDEPENDENT DECISION MAKING	☐	☐	☐
2.	GOVERN YOURSELF	☐	☐	☐
3.	ABILITY TO CONTROL ANGER	☐	☐	☐
4.	CONQUER YOURSELF	☐	☐	☐
5.	CREATIVELY HANDLE DISAPPOINTMENTS	☐	☐	☐
6.	INSPIRES CONFIDENCE	☐	☐	☐
7.	RELIABLE	☐	☐	☐
8.	CORRECTOR	☐	☐	☐
9.	MOBILIZING	☐	☐	☐
10.	CONCILIATOR	☐	☐	☐
11.	ANTAGONIZING	☐	☐	☐
12.	DEVELOP RELATIONSHIPS	☐	☐	☐
13.	UNCONDITIONAL ACCEPTANCE OF OTHERS	☐	☐	☐
14.	SELF-CONFIDENT	☐	☐	☐
15.	APPROACHABLE	☐	☐	☐
16.	EGO STRENGTH	☐	☐	☐
17.	CENTERED	☐	☐	☐
18.	FORGIVING	☐	☐	☐
19.	PURPOSEFUL	☐	☐	☐
20.	ENCOURAGING	☐	☐	☐
21.	RESPONSIBLE	☐	☐	☐

NOTES

8

QUALIFICATIONS FOR LEADERSHIP

"The quality of your character is the measure of your leadership effectiveness."

E ffective leadership is essentially built on the foundation of inspiration that breeds confidence in one's character. In its truest form it is the perfect balance of competence, vision and virtue. Competence or knowledge without vision breeds technocrats. Virtue without vision and knowledge breeds ideologies. Vision without virtue and knowledge, breeds demagogue. *True leadership cannot be divorced from the basic qualities that produce good sound character.* It involves the total person and therefore, cannot be relegated to a professional compartment of our lives.

For example, there are many who insist that their personal lives should not be linked with their professional position as a leader, and that their activities and behavior outside of their role as leader has no bearing on their ability to perform. This is a grave error and has accounted for the tragic fall of many great men and women who attempted to violate this principle of integration of the complete self.

Because leadership is a matter of inspiration based on character, then a careful understanding of the qualities that make for strong character building must be studied and embraced if you are going to exercise the capacity of quality leadership the world needs today. If the source of leadership is inspiration, and the life of leadership is confidence, then the fuel of leadership is trust. *Trust is not a gift nor a talent, but a product of time tested character forged in the midst of life's trials. A time-tested life is the raw material of character and trust. Trust must be earned.*

Leaders are not born, but are created by life. They develop the characteristics that qualifies them for a distinguished place of trustworthiness. If you want to become the leader you have the potential to become, you must commit to the qualifications presented below.

Who is better qualified to catalog the requisites of effective leadership than the peerless leader, Paul? In addition to the richness of his own experience, he enjoyed the illumination and inspiration of the Holy Spirit. Principles do not change from generation to generation, but remain constant and universal throughout time. The leadership principles and qualities presented by Paul almost two thousand years ago are as indispensable and needed as they were the day he penned them.

In every field of leadership, the church, government, civic and social, these principles are not optional extras but necessary requirements. Paul captured the heart of these qualities in his letter to a young leader he discipled, Timothy:

If anyone sets his heart on being an overseer, he desires a noble task. Now the overseer must be above reproach, the husband of but one wife, temperate, self-controlled, respectable, hospitable, able to teach, not given to much wine, not violent but gentle, not quarrelsome, not a lover of money. He must manage his own family well and see that his children obey him with proper respect. He must not be a recent convert, or he may become conceited, and fall under the same judgment as the devil. He must also have a good reputation with outsiders.

1 Timothy 3:1-7

During the political race for the presidency of the United States in 1992, the candidates, Governor Bill Clinton and President George Bush were engaged in an intense battle over personal character and moral issues. Many considered these to be less important than the position of the Presidency. However, it is evident that biblical qualifications of leadership include all aspects of the individual's character. Paul presents qualifications for leadership in six specific categories: social, ethical, temperament, maturity, intellectual and domestic. These qualities do not only characterize effective leaders, they also serve as signs of progress for all of us.

COMMITMENT TO INTEGRITY

The first category of leadership in this chapter is the commitment to integrity and high social standards. A man or woman's faithfulness will always be proven in their marriage relationship. We call people who break their marriage vows unfaithful. Faithfulness is a virtue of character. You may have talent, but you must be faithful to use it. You might be a good piano player, but if you don't show up to play, your talent is useless. Being a talented leader isn't enough, you must also be faithful.

I was teaching a group of couples who were going to be married. In our church, engaged couples go through an entire year of counseling. One of the principles I taught them was that the Bible plainly tells us that we should enjoy the wife of our youth, even in our old age. One husband for one wife.

When you can be trusted in marriage, your word can be trusted. An unfaithful partner is someone who breaks their word. When a couple gets married, words are what makes the marriage legal. Words like "I do" and "I will." A marriage contract is signed with words, your name. If one partner is unfaithful, they break their word. If you break your promise of faithfulness to your spouse, it reflects on your capacity to be faithful in a position of leadership. You must be faithful.

In a world in which moral principles come under subtle and constant attack, a leader must be blameless in that respect. He is to be faithful to his/her spouse in a society where this is far from being the norm. He must set a high standard in the marital relationship. Paul states that one who aspires to become a leader must be above reproach and of a good reputation in all circles. In essence, a leader develops a character which is not open to attack or censure.

MORAL AND ETHICAL QUALIFICATIONS

Leaders must demonstrate their commitment to the highest ideals and principles of the word of God. Never compromising the standards of truth, honesty and integrity in all walks of life.

This involves temptations that come against you as a leader. A leader must allow himself no indulgence in secrets that would undermine his character or mar his public witness.

Every time you are put in a position of responsibility, you automatically become a target for temptation. If you have a thousand people together and you put one person above the crowd, they become an easier target than if they were still in the crowd.

In other words, when you become a leader, you are put in a highly visible position and you become attractive to many interests. Why do you think leaders have to fight against the temptation of lust, bribery, financial greed or gluttony? Why? Because their position makes them more vulnerable than the others in the group.

If you want to be a leader and you cannot control your passions, wait a while before you allow yourself to be used. Be quick to hear, slow to speak and slow to get angry. That means you'll respond with gentleness and calmness the first time, the second time and the ninetieth time.

TEMPERAMENT QUALIFICATIONS

A leader must have a proper estimation of himself in Christ Jesus. His actions are then based on that estimation. Anyone who wants to be used must realize that they are like a special palace. You don't go into a palace and throw garbage around, do you? Then why would you put garbage in your palace?

I believe that our society has given in to temptation in this area. Our bodies are becoming a garbage dump. Junk food is dumped into our stomachs, smoke is dumped into our lungs, and alcohol is dumped into our kidneys and livers. If you are called to lead, you must be controlled from within and disciplined.

This applies to any habit. Some people don't drink wine but they eat too much. They don't know how to say, "No, thank you." Self-control is learning how to say, "No."

A leader must not possess a negative, violent spirit. Leaders should not be easily manipulated by the behavior or offenses of others. This means going into a rage and suddenly losing control. Have you ever heard the statement, "She made me so mad?" Do you know that nobody in the universe has the power to make you mad? I'll prove it to you. If I can make you mad, then I control you, and if I control you, then you have no control over yourself.

This also works in the opposite way. Consider the statement, "He just turns me on." Nobody can make you happy. What really happens is that you made yourself happy when you saw him. Really! You choose to be mad about what is said about you. You decide if I can make you angry or not. When people say things about me that are degrading and derogatory, I decide to stay cool. I decide that what they say is not worth getting heated up about. They can't make me mad. If a person is always under the control of others, they can't be used in leadership.

They must also be gentle or meek. Some people think that meekness is weakness. The Greek word for meekness is translated, "controlled power." Power without abuse. Gentleness means to be able to control and be wise with power. This is important, because many times, leaders are tempted to abuse power. The minute they receive authority over people, they begin to feel like they can misuse and control them. No, when you are a leader, you must be a gentle person. Wait until you have that gentle character, until you know that you have influence but you won't abuse it.

Gentleness also means that a leader won't be a show-off. They don't need to show-off because they know who they are and what they have. There are some people who are pushy. They might walk up to you and say, "Do you know who I am? I am the honorable doctor so and so with a *PHDWXYZBA* degree." Indicating that you are supposed to act a certain way when they are present. Gentleness means that you don't go walking around saying, "*I'm a Leader.*" That's not gentleness, that is insecurity.

Gentleness is like being an ambassador. Suppose the ambassador from another country walked around every day trying to convince us that he is the ambassador. He walks down the street calling, "I am the ambassador." You might think he was crazy. You know he is the ambassador, he doesn't have to tell you. He proves he is by the credentials, administration and operation of his office. Gentle people work quietly, without looking around to see who is watching them. They are not people who want others to see what they are doing. That's not gentleness, that's pride. You know that what you are doing is important, but you don't have to shout it from the rooftops.

THE QUALITY OF MATURITY

What is maturity? Maturity is the ability and quality one possesses, to accept the differences in other's opinions, views, personalities, characters, positions and status without being threatened in your own security. Maturity does not borrow strength from external circumstances nor uses them to influence or manipulate others. Maturity is the product of security.

Next, a leader must not be quarrelsome. God cannot use someone who is always in a fight. What causes quarrels? Immaturity. Do you know how hard it is to use an immature person? Always be open to learn and grow, and as you do you will be used more and more.

Maturity is indispensable to good leadership. There is no place for a novice, a new convert or inexperienced, untested character in positions of responsibility. He must not be a recent convert or he may become conceited and full of pride. If you desire to be a leader, be willing to gain experience over time and understand that you have to qualify for the trust and confidence of others. Stop rushing! You have the potential to be a leader somewhere, in some capacity, but maybe not tomorrow. All great leaders are products of time and trophies of life's wars.

A leader must also have a good reputation with outsiders. One who desires to be used in leadership has to guard his reputation. How many leaders today have good reputations?

**All great leaders are products of
time and trophies of life's wars.**

If I were to go to your job and walk around meeting the people you work with, what would they say about you? What is your reputation? I like what the Bible says about Daniel. It says they couldn't find any fault with him. He was the third highest ranking politician in the country and they tried to mar his character and reputation. They couldn't, because he had sound spiritual foundation and moral quality.

Now more than ever, we need leaders who will maintain their integrity and will not fall into disgrace or into temptation's trap. There are traps set to entangle you, now and in the future. Are you conscious of you weaknesses? Some of you may think you will evade temptation, but beware, there are traps set for you too. If you desire to be a leader, look for them. They're all around you. Guard your soul with all diligence.

One of the greatest tragedies in the world is for someone who has great potential to fall, and feel that they can never get up again. But the life of great leaders like Moses provides hope and inspiration for us all. He killed a man, he was a murderer. Yet Moses didn't stay in defeat.

Forty years after the murder, God said to him, "I want to use you." Moses replied, "You don't understand, I don't qualify, I'm not impressive, I don't have anything going for me." God said, "I want to use you anyway." Why? Because the 40 years Moses spent as a shepherd had taught him patience, leadership and how to endure hardship. He had learned enough that God said "You are the kind of man I can use." God never once mentioned the murder. I love that.

INTELLECTUAL QUALIFICATIONS

True leaders are constantly reaching for more knowledge. If you desire to become an effective leader, you must give yourself to study and never graduate from the University of Life.

How effective would it be if a geometry teacher came into the classroom and asked the students what she should teach? If the students don't know anything and the teacher doesn't know anything, how is learning going to be accomplished?

How are you going to be able to teach? You have to learn. In order to learn, you have to submit to teaching. Many people may want to be used, but they are never in a position to learn. They have all kinds of excuses why, "I've been working hard" or "I'm too busy." Then they wonder why they aren't being used effectively. You must also live the principles you have learned until they are a part of your life.

If someone were to come to me and say, "I cannot find a teacher," I wouldn't believe them. There are thousands of good, edifying books in the bookstores that can build you up and teach you. There are many people on television and radio that are teaching so you can learn and grow. Nobody in this country can ever say that they haven't had an opportunity to learn.

Those who aspire to become leaders read, they seek training, they take classes, they listen to others, they actively use both their ears and their eyes. They are curious, always asking questions. They continually expand their competence, their ability to do things. They develop new skills, new interests. They continually discover that all they know is what they have learned, and all they have learned is not all there is to know. *True leaders initiate their own learning.*

Mastery and absolute competence is mandatory for a leader. He must have a passion for more knowledge and to learn everything there is to know. *Great leaders love knowledge. They always want to know.*

FAMILY AND DOMESTIC QUALIFICATIONS

A leader must manage his family well and see that his children obey him with proper respect. A good leader will fall in love with his family, not money. A principle that I found helpful over the years has kept me conscious of my priorities in this area is this, "Do not touch the girls, the gold or the glory."

J. Oswald Sanders has this to say about a leader's family:

"The home is the test of true leadership qualification. If a man has not succeeded in exercising a benevolent and happy discipline in his own home and family, is there reason to expect that he will do better with an organizational or church family? The clear implication is, while caring for the interest for the organization, church or ministry, a true leader will not neglect the family that is his personal and primary responsibility. In the economy of God, the discharge of one God-given duty or responsibility will never involve the neglect of another."

Leadership has often been forfeited through failure in this realm. *To a leader, the family will not be sacrificed for anything.*

The leader should not be motivated by, or greedy for money, but eager to serve. That means that even if you don't pay me anything, I am happy to do the job. I am eager, excited and enthused, regardless of what you pay me. This is how we should feel, yet we know that many people do not. They say, "Unless you can pay me a certain amount, I don't want to work for you." Have a willing heart and eagerness to serve, not concerned about making a lot of money.

Also, don't "lord" over people. To "lord" means to claim a sense of ownership or to rule with a haughty spirit. There are leaders who make you feel that they own you. You can't do anything without their permission. You must give an account of where you have been and what you have been doing. In reality, you can go anywhere you want to go. As a matter of fact, we didn't ask you to read this book. You picked up this book out of your own decision, out of your own will and you are reading it by yourself. True leaders find their joy and pleasure in seeing others develop and release their own potential and become leaders themselves.

A leader must be found faithful in stewardship. A steward is someone who looks after somebody else's property. You don't own the people, they are just in your care. Be the kind of steward who leads by example.

If you cannot be a good steward of your personal resources what else can you be trusted with? If you are making $100.00 a week now, how are you handling it? That has a direct relationship with how you are going to be trusted with other things. Let's suppose you need money for a personal need and you're given that money. If you spend it on something unimportant, how can you be trusted to handle resources for someone else? Be faithful over what is given you now and then you will be trusted with more.

You must also be a good manager. The word "manage" means, the ability to coordinate and keep control. I believe people who are married and following the Lord's will often develop a new sense of responsibility or management. However, anyone who has learned to take control of their lives will be used, regardless of their marital status.

In essence, management is the coordination of energies, resources and materials toward a worthy objective. All of the above qualifications are necessary and vital for the individual who aspires to become a leader in his generation. The ability to embrace these qualities lies within your reach and I encourage you to get your life on a course to develop these qualities and give your generation an exceptional leader to emulate.

Real leadership power comes
from a honorable character.

PRINCIPLES

1. Effective leadership is the perfect balance of competence, vision and virtue.

2. If the source of leadership is inspiration, and the life of leadership is confidence, then the fuel of leadership is trust.

3. A leader should be above reproach.

4. The character of a leader should be one that commands respect from all, even his enemies.

5. A leader must allow himself no indulgence in secrets that would undermine his character or mar his public witness.

6. A leader must have wisdom.

7. Mastery, absolute confidence, is mandatory for a leader.

8. A leader must be a gentle person.

9. A leader must manage his family well.

10. The leader should not be motivated by, or greedy for money.

11. If you desire to be a leader, be willing to gain experience over time and understand that you have to qualify for the trust and confidence of others.

QUALIFICATIONS FOR LEADERSHIP

1. SOCIAL
2. ETHICAL
3. TEMPERAMENT
4. MATURITY
5. INTELLECTUAL
6. DOMESTIC

NOTES

ESSENTIAL QUALITIES OF LEADERSHIP

"The heights by great men reached and kept were not attained by sudden flight; but they, while their companions slept, were toiling upward in the night."

Although we are each born with God-given and unique personality traits, there are common characteristics that must be present in the life of a leader. The following are a few of these characteristics.

DISCIPLINE

You must be disciplined. This is the heart of leadership development. Discipline requires decision. If you need help establishing discipline in your life, ask for it, but don't stop there. Once you ask for help, take the advice given to you and change your actions. This world needs leaders who are disciplined people.

Discipline means obedience, and imposing strict guidelines on yourself. Don't let someone else set guidelines for you, rather, discipline yourself.

The highest form of discipline is self-discipline, and only those who have excelled in this quality will rise to the surface of life and demand the respect of others. Only the self-disciplined have earned the right to discipline others.

VISION

You must possess a guiding vision. Throughout history the greatest leaders of the world were "seers." That is somebody who could see beyond what everybody else was looking at. You can see what's down the road, and you can see what it's going to take to get there. Some people have foresight, but they have no insight, and they fall short of quality leadership. Visionaries are people who are not satisfied with what's happening, but who are interested in what's going to happen and how they can make it happen. Some people go with the flow, but visionaries create their own. Be a visionary, even if you seem to be an oddball.

Without a vision, people perish. You've got to have a vision. It imparts adventure. As Westerners, we've been taught that you grow up, go to school, get married and just wait until your name is called before you step out and become productive. For years you sit around waiting to hear your name called. There's work to do. People are falling into destruction every day. There are thousands to be helped. We have many different tools at our disposal to accomplish this, but we are just sitting around. We have no vision.

Always move in your vision. That means the willingness to take fresh steps into the light. There are those who say faith is a leap in the dark. Not so! I'm not going into the dark, I take great leaps into the light.

Some people start moving in their vision and they go a long way. Then they look back and say, "Look how far I have come. Isn't that wonderful?" Five years later they are saying, "Do you want to see how far I've come?" Twenty years later, they are asking the same thing. In thirty years, they still haven't made any more progress.

A leader is somebody who could see beyond what everybody else was looking at.

You may be facing a problem thinking, "I'm never going to get out of this one." Remember the problems you've gotten out of in the past? They came and they went. So when problems come, look at them and say, "It's all right. I know you'll go away, too." There's nothing in this world that is not temporary.

A vision without a task makes a visionary. A task without a vision is drudgery. Some people have visions without the will to bring them into reality.

They dream but they don't wake up. I know some people that have great ideas and they talk to everyone about them, then they go back home and sit. They say, "It'd be nice to go to college, get a degree and open a business. Wouldn't it be great?" They talk and talk and when they finish, they go back home, sit down and cross their legs. That's a visionary who has no mission. A missionary is somebody who has a vision and puts that vision to work.

When I first decided that I was going to get my B.A. I thought that was the farthest thing from me. I was back home thinking, "No one in my family has ever attended college. What am I doing even thinking about it?" But I began to keep company with God and I began to think, "school," but it didn't end there. I had to start with my GED. That's putting the vision and the task together. I became an academic missionary. I began to study when everybody else was playing. I was reading algebra when everybody else was eating lunch. It took work.

I got my GED and I thought I'd accomplished something big. I said, "Ready now, Lord?" And he said, "No. Entrance exams." I said, "Oh, no!" So I started putting my nose to the grindstone again. I studied and I studied and I studied, and I passed. Then the Lord said, "Well, you wanted a B.A., now you have to go to a university." I thought, "Oh, no, four years of my life." Four years seemed like a long time at first, but they went by fast.

When I finished I thought, "I've got a B.A. now, let's get a master's degree. I worked at bettering myself. I overcame. I looked back and thought, "What was impossible became possible," and my mind began to open. When you have tasted possibilities, it is very difficult to settle for impossibilities.

When you have tasted possibilities, it is very difficult to settle for impossibilities.

A vision is a glimpse of the end, a view of your purpose in life. Vision is like the finished product that you are about to produce. Leaders keep their hands on the potters wheel but their eyes on the finished product. This is Vision. Vision is the source of discipline and self-motivation. Have you found a guiding vision to fill your days with life?

Many people are going through life with no idea of where they will end up. If you could sit down right now with a blank sheet of paper, and set goals for your life, you will find that you will accomplish more. A plan and goals will give you direction. Everybody's looking, but only those people who are conscious of their purpose and possess a guiding vision will truly see.

COMMON SENSE

This is sometimes called wisdom. Wisdom is the ability to use knowledge effectively. It suggests a safe perspective on life, a sense of balance, a clear understanding of how the various parts and principles apply and relate to each other and the whole. It consists of judgment, discernment, comprehension, insight, hindsight, and foresight. It is oneness, and integrated wholeness. Wisdom protects knowledge from abuse. Proverbs 4:7 says "Wisdom is supreme, therefore get wisdom. Though it cost you all you have, get understanding."

Some people are so smart that they have no common sense. Once I was flying to Miami and I tried to talk with the lady sitting next to me. I said, "Good evening." and she said, "Praise the Lord." I said, "Nice weather." And she said, "Glory to God." I asked, "What's your name?" and she said, "Thank you Jesus." "Where are you going?" "Bless God, hallelujah, glory to God, I'm going to Miami, praise God."

"What are you going to do there?" "Well, thank you, Jesus, by the grace of God, when I get there, glory to God and with His mercy and the angels guarding me, I'll go into Miami praise the Lord, thank you, Jesus. He'll walk me down to the store, hallelujah, glory to God. I'll buy a pair of shoes, thank you Jesus, and if His grace follows with me and goodness and mercy behind me, thank you Lord, I'll buy a dress, praise Jesus."

I was sitting there thinking, "Lady, let's just talk. Let's just converse." She had knowledge of the word and she had a relationship with Jesus, but she had no wisdom. Wisdom is the ability to use what you have, and use it effectively. God is not moved by your impressions of Christianity, he wants to see you live the relevance of Christ. ***Wisdom is a combination of discernment, judgment and tact.*** You have to deal with people where they're at.

Too many times we become wise after the fact. After we've gotten into trouble, we turn around and say, "I shouldn't have done that." That's wisdom too late.

Wisdom is the ability to make use of knowledge effectively.

We need leaders who are wise, not smart-alecks. Smart-alecks are people who don't know, but they make you believe they do. A wise man knows, but he doesn't have to prove it to you. I spoke to a man once who had a college degree, but he just couldn't seem to get along with others on the job. He had knowledge but no wisdom to know how to relate to them. Wisdom should not be confused with education.

Wisdom is more precious than rubies, and nothing you desire can compare with it. That means you can receive the greatest academic honor, and still be dumb. Wisdom is more important than academic accomplishments. Do you want to be a leader? Go after wisdom, discipline and understanding.

Wisdom is the ability to make use of knowledge effectively. Many people have knowledge, but not all have common sense. Many people have information, but they have no revelation. Activate common sense.

The scriptures teach that wisdom comes from above. The source of wisdom is God. Therefore, a leader must have a dynamic relationship with the source of wisdom and contact with him daily.

DECISIVENESS

You must be decisive. Be a decision maker! Let your yes be yes and your no be no. Anything more than this is evil. Your life is dependent on the two words yes and no. When you are in a decision, a tight spot with temptation, the easiest thing to do is to say, "Well, maybe it'll go away." That won't work, it's either yes or no. Make a decision. Then stick with your decision and accept the consequences.

A leader must be willing to be decisive because he knows that indecision is a decision not to decide. It is better to make a decision that may not be the best, than to not make one at all. Lead decisively.

FORTITUDE

You must be courageous. Many people do not have any moral fortitude. They fall under every new temptation: lust, greed, fear, etc. They have no control or integrity. What would you do if you were confronted with moral temptation? Some people sacrifice their morals for personal gain or reputation.

What is the definition of courage? J. Oswald Sanders defines courage as, "the quality of mind which enables men to encounter danger and difficulty with firmness, and without fear or depression." A leader who is fickle or critical cannot be used. If you have to talk to your boss about something that's on your mind, do you think about it for twelve months, get to his door, then say, "Let's think about this some more." Or do you go right in and with an attitude of respect and speak your mind? Be courageous. Some people are afraid to apply courage because they already believe they're going to be turned down or they're going to fail.

**Courage is resistance to and mastery
of fear, not the absence of fear.**

For years and years I used to pray for strength and guess what, I never got an ounce. Why? Because all the strength you need, you already have. Courage is standing up on your strength. Courage is resistance to and mastery of fear, not the absence of fear. All leaders encounter the complexity of fear, but they are never immobilized by it, they use it to motivate their potential. This is courage.

Do you know where your strength comes from? Joy. You can't pray for strength before you find your joy. What happens in this world is not supposed to touch your joy, true joy comes from within. Joy is the secret of our strength. Courage is something that you already have, just be courageous. One man with courage is a majority. The scars you acquire by exercising courage will never make you feel inferior. Courage is doing what you're afraid to do. There can be no courage unless you're scared. Be of good courage. It is the mark of true leadership.

HUMILITY

You must be humble. If you want to be a leader, you need a mixture of courage and strength tempered with humility. What is humility? Humility is the ability to be yourself. Humility is from the root word, humus, meaning earth, from where we derive our word, human. Thus, humility denotes earthiness, or awareness of one's true essence.

Humility, therefore, is not the degrading or reducing of oneself in the estimation of another, but rather the awareness, acceptance and appreciation of one's true worth and value. In this regard, you cannot decide to be humble, because it is not something you decide to be, it is what you are. True leaders are individuals who have discovered their true selves and knows who they are. Thus, *true leaders are naturally humble.*

Humility is the ability to control power.

Humility is also the ability to transfer glory. In other words, you are not so uptight about receiving all of the recognition that you can't acknowledge someone else's contribution. You can say, "His help made it possible." John the Baptist displayed great humility in his declaration, "He must become greater; I must become less." (John 3:30).

Yet humility is not stupidity. It doesn't mean that you allow yourself to be pressured to do something because someone puts you on a guilt trip. There are some wives whose husbands abuse them physically, they take advantage of them, and then the wives say, "I've got to stay humble." That's not humility, that's dumb. Humility is the ability to control knowledge and power, even though you know it's yours to exercise. Speak your knowledge at the right time, in the right words and to the right person.

If you have to say, "I'm humble," you're not. When somebody tells you that they're humble, it is proof that they are proud. Proof of your humility is when someone else tells you, "You know, I like you. You don't think yourself above anybody. You esteem others higher than yourself." Humility is a quality of character that is a result of God's love and mercy in your life. When I realize what God has done for me, there's no way I can think of myself as being higher than you, because what he did for me, he'll do for you.

A humble leader will be willing to take on the job nobody wants. If something needs to be done, a leader with humility will step in and do it. He'll do it with joy and as best as he can, because he understands the importance of that job getting done.

**Humility is knowing who you are
and accepting it without boasting.**

There is a good example of this in scripture. Before Jesus was arrested, he and the disciples had their last meal together. It was a custom in those days, that before a meal was served, a servant washed the feet of the arriving guests. There were no servants when Jesus and the disciples arrived for dinner, but their feet needed to be washed just the same.

I can see the disciples arguing among themselves about who would do this menial task. As they were arguing, Jesus took a towel and a wash basin and began to do the job. The disciples were stunned into silence. Not only did the job get done, but they learned a valuable lesson of the true meaning of leadership. *Humility is knowing who you are and accepting it without boasting.*

SENSE OF HUMOR

You must cultivate a strong sense of humor. The ability to laugh in life and not take life too seriously is a gift from our Creator. Psalms 2:4 states, "The one enthroned in heaven laughs." The gift of humor and laughter is a characteristic and quality of God's nature. Since we are created in the image of God, this gift is a natural component of our nature and should play an active role in our fulfillment.

Humor is an asset to the leader and helps in maintaining a proper perspective in life. The spirit of the true leader is always cheerful, pleasant, happy, upbeat, optimistic, positive and open. With a healthy sense of humor, leaders can transform a tense situation unto a positive environment, and create an atmosphere of understanding.

I went to preach in a little town right outside Tulsa, Oklahoma in 1974. It seemed like I was the only black man in this little town. They didn't see black folks in that area very often and the only thing they really knew about blacks was that they were once slaves. I was invited there by a professor who wanted me to preach in a church. When I stood up, all I saw were white faces. They had come to see this young man from Oral Roberts University, and then they realize, he's black. I could feel the tension. They figure that only white people go to Oral Roberts, and then the school sent me.

As I stood up there with all those beautiful faces looking at me, they didn't know what to do. They were nervous. So, I stood up and said, "Do you all know how I feel? I feel like a raisin in a bowl of corn flakes." They laughed and they laughed till they couldn't laugh anymore. When they were finished, I started to preach and everything was all right. When I was through preaching, we had about sixteen people come forward to give their hearts to God. They invited me back three times to preach in that same church, and they invited all the other churches to come hear me. It was exciting.

You have to have the ability to laugh at yourself. That's so important. Some people are too hard on themselves. Have you ever slipped and fallen in front of people? What do you do? Get up and laugh with them and say, "Ah, did you see what I just did? Isn't that funny, I just fell down." Laugh, because if that were somebody else, you would have laughed.

A merry heart makes a cheerful face. If your heart is merry you'll notify your face. All the days of the oppressed are wretched, but the cheerful have continual peace. A merry heart is good like medicine, but a crushed and broken spirit cause a dryness of the bones. What do you take medicine for? To get well when you're sick. Who is joy a medicine for? If you aren't sick, you could go to somebody who is depressed, downhearted and broken, and as a leader, you could take them out of that with a smile and some humor.

It's difficult for you to smile and not get one in return. A smile is something that you can't buy, you can't bribe someone for it, and it's no good to you. *A good leader must have a sense of humor.*

INDIGNATION

You must possess the quality of anger. Leaders who have impacted their generation did so only after they got angry at injustice and abuse among men. Compassion itself is a product of anger against what hurts humanity.

You've got to hate wrongdoing. Hate it so much that when you see it, it makes you mad. That's the kind of indignation you should have. I get angry when I see young people being destroyed by drugs. I hate it. I love those young people, but I hate that which is killing them. *A true leader hates the things God hates.* Jesus himself possessed this quality as is demonstrated in John 2:15-17 "Jesus looked on them with anger."

PATIENCE AND ENDURANCE

You must possess the quality of patience and endurance. William Barclay explains and defines patience:

"This word never means the spirit that sits with folded hands and simply bears things. It is victorious endurance, constancy under trial. It is steadfastness, the brave and courageous acceptance of everything life can do to us, and the transforming of even the worst circumstance into another step on the upward way. It is the courageous and triumphant ability to bear things, which enables

man to pass the breaking point without breaking and to always greet the unseen with a cheer."

It also means the ability to allow room for others to fail and be different. Paul wrote, "We who are strong ought to bear with the failings of the weak." (Romans 15:1) The man who is impatient with weakness will be defective in his leadership.

True leaders do not overreact to negative behaviors, criticism, or human weakness. They don't feed on the weakness of others. They realize that behavior and potential are two different things. They believe in the unseen potential of all people and always see beyond the weakness. They believe in the ability of others to change.

FELLOWSHIP AND FRIENDSHIP

All true leaders are friendly and open to inviting others into their lives. They are not afraid to extend themselves to others because of their security. They are easy to befriend because they are confident in their self worth and can share themselves without fear.

The commitment of true leaders to inspire and help others to become the best they can be, and to maximize their full potential makes them attractive to many. *Leaders posses the faculty of being able to attract and draw the best out of other people.*

Jesus was the ultimate example of this quality. He expressed the value of his friends in his life. Remember, a true friend is one who brings out the best in you.

DISCRETION

You must cultivate the quality of tact and diplomacy. Leaders must be tactful and diplomatic. They must possess the ability to communicate their thoughts without causing offenses. "The wise in heart are called discerning, and pleasant words promote instruction." (Proverbs 16:21) If you want to help someone who's hurting, don't speak to him with words that offend him, rather, lift him up with kindness, diplomacy and tact.

Proverbs 16:23, "A wise man's heart guides his mouth, and his lips promote instruction." Have you ever heard, "I'm going to give you a piece of my mind?" That's not what people need, they need a piece of your heart. The Bible says, "Out of the good treasure of your heart, come good works." Give people the treasure that's in your heart and you'll be a tactful leader.

To become an effective leader, you must be able to conduct delicate negotiations and matters in a way that enhances mutual rights and yet leads to a harmonious solution. Leaders know that the key to having influence with others is when others know that they have influence with you.

When Peter denied Jesus, Jesus could have been brutal and rebuked him, but instead he was very tactful. After his resurrection, he instructed Mary to go and get the disciples and he made sure that Peter was included. He knew Peter had done wrong, he knew that Peter had failed him, yet he acted as if it had never happened.

Proverbs 17:27, "A man of knowledge uses words with restraint, and a man of understanding is even tempered." Restraint means that you may want to express your displeasure in no uncertain terms, but you don't. Someone may deserve it but a wise and knowledgeable man won't do it, even if he feels like it. Effective leaders always go for the win/win option because they respect the value of all men.

INSPIRATIONAL POWER

You must be able to inspire others. The ability to inspire others to serve and sacrifice is the mark of a true leader. Inspiration is the capacity to mobilize, activate, motivate, stimulate and cause others by your own character and zeal for a passionate vision, to participate in a change of their own priorities. It encourages people to keep moving.

The above qualities are essential, required and time-tested for truly efficient and exceptional leadership. Your capacity for becoming a leader is unlimited if you are willing to commit to refining, developing and appropriating all of these vital principles into your life. Remember, true character is made in secret and displayed openly.

The man who is impatience with weakness will be defective in his leadership.

PRINCIPLES

1. A leader is a person who has first submitted willingly and learned to obey a discipline imposed from without, but who then imposes on himself a much more rigorous discipline from within.

2. Leaders are men of faith, for faith is vision.

3. Wisdom is more important than academic accomplishments.

4. When all the relevant facts are in, a swift and clear decision is the mark of a true leader.

5. Courage is resistance to and mastery of fear, not the absence of fear.

6. Humility is the ability to transfer glory.

7. A leader must be able to reconcile opposing viewpoints without giving offense and without compromising principle.

8. In order to lead, it is essential that we are led by the Spirit of God.

9. True character is made in secret and is displayed openly.

ESSENTIAL QUALITIES FOR LEADERSHIP

1. DISCIPLINE
2. VISION
3. COMMON SENSE
4. DECISIVENESS
5. FORTITUDE
6. HUMILITY
7. SENSE OF HUMOR
8. INDIGNATION
9. PATIENCE AND ENDURANCE
10. FELLOWSHIP
11. DISCRETION
12. INSPIRATIONAL POWER

NOTES

10

THE PRICE OF LEADERSHIP

*True leaders transcend private
comforts to comfort others.*

Anyone who aspires to the position of leadership must not be misguided by the perceived glory, prominence and benefits of such an honorable position. True leadership always demands a high price of the leader, and the more effective the leadership is, the higher the price to be paid. Jesus expressed this component of leadership in His warning question to His ambitious disciples, "Can you drink the cup I drink or be baptized with the baptism that I am baptized with?" (Mark 10:38).

In speaking of His own leadership cost, Jesus declared to his disciples, "whoever wants to become great among you must be your servant, and whoever wants to be first must be slave of all. For even the Son of Man did not come to be served, but to serve, and to give His life as a ransom for many" (Mark 10:44-45).

If you desire to accept the challenge of leadership and to impact your generation, you must be prepared to accept and face the cost that comes with leadership responsibility. There are countless challenges and trials that leaders must endure, but in this chapter we will look at some of the common ones that all effective leaders must face.

PERSONAL SACRIFICE

Leadership demands a commitment of service to others, a placing of the needs of others above our own. Because true leadership is born out of a guiding vision and a passion to accomplish a noble task, and to inspire others to develop and release their potential, it derives its fulfillment from the success of others.

Any leadership that is preoccupied with the elevation of its own status, glory and objectives, is not true leadership. True leaders are willing to lay down their lives for objectives that are greater than their own personal well-being. Paul expressed this aspect of leadership in his statement, "let no one cause me trouble, for I bear on my body the marks of Jesus" (Galatians 6:17). Jesus established the price of self-sacrifice in leadership in His statement, "Whoever finds his life will lose it, and whoever loses his life for my sake will find it" (Matthew 10:39).

If you will become the leader you were born to be, you cannot escape the price of self-sacrifice. Remember, true leaders have not only found a purpose and objective to live for, but they have found a vision to die for. You will never change life in your generation until you are willing to die for that change. Greatness in life is found in the willingness to die.

REJECTION

One of the most common costs of leadership is the experience of rejection. If you are willing to accept the call to leadership in your generation, you must be willing to be rejected and misunderstood by all.

This price was paid by the ultimate leader, Jesus Christ, as seen by his reception in his own community, "He came to that which was his own, but his own did not receive him" (John 1:11). It is said, no man is ever fully accepted until he has first of all, been utterly rejected. If you depend on or need the agreement of everyone around you in order to feel secure, you will never be a successful and effective leader. True leaders affect change, and change by its very nature engenders conflict and resistance.

Leadership is the projection of one's life, and as you lead you will inevitably encounter opposition. It is also true, that often great leaders are never appreciated nor recognized by their contemporaries, rather by following generations. Rejection does not mean you are wrong, but it does indicate that you are challenging others to change. Remember, blessed are those who are persecuted for righteousness sake (Matthew 5:10).

CRITICISM

All leaders can identify with this reality. Criticism is a way of life for leadership. No leader is exempt. The very nature of effective leadership involves taking a position on issues, making decisions and determining direction. These will always result in some form of reaction from one's environment, usually negative.

However, it should also be understood that true leaders are not affected by criticism, and would, in most cases see it as a positive opportunity to test their conviction and commitment. Criticism is usually the manifestation of jealousy, insecurity or fear, and should be seen as a normal, human response to action.

Criticism is the leader's greatest test of maturity, conviction and commitment to his vision. If you are ready for criticism, you're ready for leadership.

If you do not want to be criticized, then decide to do nothing in life. It is better to be criticized for action than to be ignored for non-action. Criticism is the leader's greatest test of maturity, conviction and commitment to his vision. If you are ready for criticism, you're ready for leadership. Remember the words of Jesus, "Blessed are you when people insult you, persecute you and falsely say all kinds of evil against you because of me. Rejoice and be glad, because great is your reward in heaven, for in the same way they persecuted the prophets who were before you" (Matthew 5:11-12). Criticism is not new or unique, it is common to all effective leadership.

LONELINESS

Leadership is lonely, because to lead means you must be out in front, ahead of the followers. Also, because the leader is the one with the guiding vision and purpose, he sees the end from the beginning and must live both the process and destination, all at the same time.

There is also the responsibility for decision making that falls on the leader. Despite the fact that a good leader delegates, he is also aware that there are decisions only he can make that will effect the lives of many. This is a lonely path. The loneliest person today is the one who has been entrusted with a message, dream or vision, that is ahead of his time or conflicts with the accepted norm.

Great leaders, both men and women, who have changed the world and impacted their generation, were lonely souls. Though the life of a leader may be filled with people, he must tread a lonely path, for this is the price and nature of leadership. Jesus was forsaken by all of his disciples in his greatest hour of need, yet he stood and saw his purpose fulfilled. *If you are not willing to stand alone in your vision, not many will be willing to stand with you.*

PRESSURE AND PERPLEXITY

Leaders must face the inevitable challenge of the responsibilities and demands that come with leader-

ship. These involve the need to make critical decisions, and often under time constraints and external
pressure. The leader must weigh all the issues,
information and opinions and make the best possible
decision. This can be perplexing and exact a heavy toll
on his emotional, psychological and physical capacity. It may even become a source of temporary stress
and must be managed. This is a price of leadership
and must be expected.

Few followers can ever appreciate this costly responsibility upon the leader. There are times when
even as a Christian leader, it seems like God is not
speaking to you and you are left to make critical
decisions from your experience and knowledge of the
Word and Biblical principles. This is the measure of
the leaders maturity in Christ. Remember, purpose
has its perplexity. Jesus experienced this price in the
Garden of Gethsemane as he struggled with the
decision that would affect the future of the entire
world.

MENTAL AND PHYSICAL FATIGUE

Leadership places heavy demands on the individual
who fills the position. There is no way to become an
effective leader and not be affected by its stress,
physical demands and mental toll. All leaders must
possess an exceptional degree of stamina and physical
energy if they are to effectively motivate and inspire
others.

The effect of your enthusiasm upon your people should be the contagious influence of positive energy. It is said that, "the world is run by tired men," and that men and women who change the world do not love sleep. *If you are willing to work harder, longer, more intense and beyond the call of duty, you will become an effective leader.*

For this reason, a true leader will incorporate in his life and be committed to a physical health program and diet plan. He also maintains a close relationship with his source, the Heavenly Father to whom he retreats often in quiet prayer and solitude to have his soul restored. Even Jesus found cause to retreat and rest. He stole away on many occasions from the stress of the large crowds to the quiet refuge of prayer with His Father. *If you are willing to pay the price of fatigue, then you are willing to lead.*

PRICE PAID BY OTHERS

If you want to be a leader, you must be aware of the tremendous cost which will be born by those closest to you. Because leadership demands the giving of oneself to others, his life becomes the property of those whom he serves. Therefore, no true leader can expect to live a normal life as other people do. His time is not his own. His gifts, talents and experience are employed and deployed in service to others. This has a direct effect and impact on his family, spouse, close friends and others dear to him.

The leader must be careful to strike a balance between serving the people and meeting his family responsibilities and other obligations. Jesus found himself in this dilemma and had to say to his earthly parents, "'Why were you searching for me?' he asked. 'Didn't you know I had to be in my Father's house?'" (Luke 2:49). If you're not willing to share your family and loved ones with others, then you will not be effective in leadership. *Leaders belong to their generation and not to themselves.*

> *True leaders cultivate character with the fertilizer of self discipline.*

PRINCIPLES

1. If you desire to accept the challenge of leadership and to impact your generation, you must be prepared to accept and face the cost that comes with leadership responsibility.

2. Criticism is a way of life for leadership.

3. If you are not willing to stand alone in your vision, not many will be willing to stand with you.

4. If you are willing to pay the price of fatigue, then you are willing to lead.

THE PRICE OF LEADERSHIP

1. PERSONAL SACRIFICE
2. REJECTION
3. CRITICISM
4. LONELINESS
5. PRESSURE AND PERPLEXITY
6. MENTAL AND PHYSICAL FATIGUE
7. PRICE PAID BY OTHERS

11

THE DANGERS OF LEADERSHIP

True leaders possess the horizon perspective and a frontier spirit.

Even though the aspiration to leadership is described as "an honorable ambition" by the great leader, Paul, you must also be made aware of the hazards and dangers of leadership. Paul, who was also aware of these perils wrote a reminder to himself in the words, "...so that after I have preached to others, I myself will not be disqualified..." (I Corinthians 9:27). We will discuss briefly, a few of the more common dangers to maintaining authentic and effective leadership.

POPULARITY

Leadership, by its conspicuous nature, lends itself to the development of the "cult of personality." One of the greatest dangers to a leader is to encourage and embrace the over-estimation of themselves by their followers, to the point where they themselves become the focus of attention. The true leader will constantly protect himself from this temptation by focusing the affection of his followers on the Lord Jesus Christ, and the vision to which He has called them.

The practice of undue deference to leaders was warned against by Paul in his letter to the church at Corinth when he wrote, "For when one says, 'I follow Paul,' and another, 'I follow Apollos,' are you not mere men? What, after all, is Apollos? And what is Paul? Only servants, through whom you came to believe - as the Lord has assigned to each his task...For we are God's fellow workers" (I Corinthians 3:4-9).

Any measure of success exposes a man to the pressure of people and therefore, tempts him to compromise his values, convictions and integrity to maintain this popularity. This has been the down-fall of many great leaders and was, in fact, a manifestation of the presence or development of insecurity. *A leader who knows who he is, does not depend on others to validate his sense of self-worth.* He also understands that any measure of popularity is simply a temporary reaction of people to his gifts and position, and not the maintenance of his person. *True leaders do not confuse applause with affirmation.*

PRIDE

Leadership naturally raises an individual to a position of prominence and significance in the eyes of many, and therefore, tends to encourage a secret self-congratulation and over-estimation of himself. This is the foundation of pride. It comes from believing the praise of men as the true measure of your worth.

Pride is very deceptive and difficult to detect by the one who possesses it, yet must be abhorred. The Scriptures have strong words to say about this dangerous culprit, "The Lord detests all the proud of heart. Be sure of this: They will not go unpunished" (Proverbs 16:5). Pride is usually evidence of a poor self-concept and low self-esteem.

Pride is usually evidence of a poor self-concept and low self-esteem.

It is the need to elevate one's self by the devaluation of others. It is the attempt to secure a sense of superiority by the maintenance of the feeling of inferiority in others. True leaders are constantly aware that they are privileged to serve and owe any measure of success or accomplishment to God and the cooperation of others. *True leaders never forget from whence they came, and live to bring others to where they are.* Paul reminds us all, never to think of ourselves more highly than we ought (Romans 12:3). Be yourself and nothing else.

EGOTISM AND INDISPENSABILITY

One of the greatest dangers to leaders is the temptation to measure all others by oneself. This is the practice of magnifying and elevating oneself and one's attainment. It's the sense of exaggerated self-importance. He considers everything in relation to himself. Egotism is a manifestation of pride and insecurity. This leads to the second and related temptation, the belief that one is indispensable. This is the temptation to think that you are irreplaceable and that the success of everything depends on you.

This is a great danger to those who have been magnified by the followers and believes that he is the only one with a monopoly on success. *True leaders are always aware that they are only a link in a long, historical chain.* They are given the privilege and brief opportunity to serve their generation with the gifts they have received, and they are obligated to prepare others to replace themselves. They esteem others above themselves and seek their good. These two perils must be avoided at all costs.

JEALOUSY

It is natural to measure the success of leadership by the accomplishment of its objectives. However, there is a temptation to measure one's success by *comparison* to the accomplishments of others. This is dangerous and is the birth of a jealous spirit. The jealous person is apprehensive and suspicious of rivals. The *true leader does not measure his success by comparing himself with others, but with his own purpose and vision.*

If you are sure of your own assignment in life, then you are free from competition, comparison and thus, jealousy. Guard your heart and mind against this vile spirit of deceit and envy, because there is only one who can do what you were born to do, and God will not reward you for competition, but for obedience to your own vision.

DISQUALIFICATION

The greatest and most common peril of leadership is that of disqualifying oneself from the position of leadership. It is the responsibility of the leader to secure the trust, confidence and commitment of his followers by adhering to the moral, ethical and spiritual principles discussed in this book. It is also his responsibility to guard against the dangers mentioned above.

It is essential that the true leader be vigilant in guarding his heart, mind and life from any compromise that would render him untrustworthy and unrespectable in the sight of all. He must adhere to the highest principles of honor, integrity, morality and self-respect. He must commit to impose spiritual standards and disciplines on himself, so that there would be no need for imposition of external discipline.

Today, we need leaders who will provide the quality of character, the standards of grace and the image of holiness, righteousness and faithfulness to God's principles and precepts, that would inspire others to desire to become leaders of exceptional quality.

Our world today is suffering a leadership vacuum, but you can change it. You have within you the ability, capacity and power to become a change agent in this generation. Don't wait for someone else to take responsibility for the future. You do it now! Rise up from the seat of the follower, and enter the school of leadership, for it is God's will that you lead others to their full potential in Him. Settle for nothing less than your best. We need you! If you accept this challenge, then read this book again until you are filled with the desire to lead others to leadership.

THE KIND OF LEADER TO BE

I encourage you to continually strive to develop your full leadership potential, and to become the following:

BE A RESPONSIBLE LEADER
BE A GROWING LEADER
BE AN EXEMPLARY LEADER
BE AN INSPIRING LEADER
BE AN EFFICIENT LEADER
BE A CARING LEADER
BE A COMMUNICATING LEADER
BE A GOAL-ORIENTED LEADER
BE A DECISIVE LEADER
BE A WORKING LEADER
BE A UNIFYING LEADER
BE A COMPETENT LEADER
BE A LEADER LED BY THE GREAT LEADER OF
  LEADERS, JESUS CHRIST!

Leaders see the world
while others see the village.

PRINCIPLES

1. A leader who knows who he is, does not depend on others to validate his sense of self-worth.

2. True leaders never forget from whence they came, and live to bring others to where they are.

3. True leaders are always aware that they are only a link in a long, historical chain.

4. The true leader does not measure his success by comparing himself with others, but with his own purpose and vision.

5. It is essential that the true leader be vigilant in guarding his heart, mind and life from any compromise that would render him untrustworthy and unrespectable in the sight of all.

THE DANGERS OF LEADERSHIP

1. POPULARITY
2. PRIDE
3. EGOTISM AND INDISPENSABILITY
4. JEALOUSY
5. DISQUALIFICATION

12

A WORD TO THE THIRD WORLD

The quality of tomorrow's leaders lie in the character of today's followers.

Today there are over five billion people on planet earth. Over half of these people live in countries and conditions that have been labeled *third world*. This term was invented by a French economist who was attempting to describe the various groupings of people throughout the world based on their socio-economic status. Whether or not this term is valid, it is generally accepted as a description or element of identification for millions of people.

I was born and live in a part of the world that is said to fall within this category. The term is identified as any people who did not benefit from or participate in the industrial revolution. A large majority of these people were not allowed to benefit from the industrial revolution because they were subjugated at the time, being used to fuel the economic base for the revolution. Many of them were reduced to slaves and indentured servants, thus robbing them of their identity, dignity, self-worth and self-respect.

However, despite the changes in conditions and a greater measure of freedom and independence, many of these peoples are still grappling with their identity and their sense of self-worth. Many of the nations that progressed and developed through the industrial revolution have reinforced (by attitude, policies, and legislation) the notion that these third world peoples do not possess the potential to develop the skills, intelligence and sophistication necessary to equal that of industrialized states.

With this prejudice and misconception in mind, I wish to say to all third World peoples everywhere; African, Indian, Latin, Oriental and other nationalities - your potential is limitless and cannot be measured by the opinions of others. You possess the ability to achieve, develop, accomplish, produce, create and perform anything your mind can conceive. God created you with all the potential you need to fulfill your purpose in this life.

ZEAL WITHOUT SKILL

Historically, the Third World peoples have always been a hard-working, dedicated, zealous and highly sensitive people. Many of them are products of oppression and have had instilled in them a sense of timidity, lack of self-confidence and a spirit of dependency. They fail in many cases to realize the capacity of the leadership potential within them.

In most of these Third World countries, the system of colonialism and the process of colonization carried with it the dehumanizing element of fostering dependency and robbing individuals of the essential aspect of creative development. This debilitating system also provided its subjects with basic training for service but not for productivity.

In essence, they were taught how to grow sugar cane, but not how to make sugar; they were taught how to grow cotton but not how to make cloth. The result was a perpetuation of dependency, for even after they were "liberated," or as some call it "emancipated," they were left with the raw material but no ability to transform it into end products.

In effect they were left with the zeal of freedom without the skill for development. This is the reason why so many of our Third World nations today are still experiencing tremendous hardship and turmoil. The industrialized states that once colonized them have maintained a sense of control and superiority that manifests itself in a sophisticated form of economic colonialism instead of political colonialism.

The Third World nations in effect are led to still look to the industrially developed states for their measure of standard, quality and excellence. This in turn breeds a sense of disrespect and suspicion for their own products and a denial of the great potential that lies dormant in these great people everywhere.

This distrust of and denial of potential was also transferred to the church world through mission efforts. Many churches throughout Third World countries are products of foreign based missions and in most cases were dependent on a "mother" church organization. This dependency factor continued even to the time of national independence, leaving many of these ministries without well trained, confident, competent and skilled leaders.

Even to this day, despite the fact that many of these church organizations have qualified and capable leaders, there is still the notion that the presence of a foreign element is necessary for the maintenance of excellence and quality.

However, there is a fresh wind of responsibility blowing throughout these Third World countries stirring a sense of destiny and purpose in the hearts of these people everywhere. This awakening of the spirit of responsibility is being felt in all arenas, political, social, civic and spiritual. It is therefore imperative that the Third World people look to the inner strength and potential lying deep within them, and with a renewed commitment to the Creator, Jesus Christ, and prepare themselves for the refinement of skills. The book of Ecclesiastes 10:10 states:

"If the axe is dull and its edge unsharpened, more strength is needed but skill will bring success."

It is my desire that every man, woman, boy and girl in every nation and every race come to realize the tremendous potential and capacity for greatness that lies dormant within them.

TRUE LEADERSHIP IS FREEDOM

No man is truly free until every man is free. This is the essence of life and the goal of leadership. Much of what we call freedom is not freedom at all, but simply permission given by an oppressor to become somebody. This is not freedom. If the source of your liberty is another person or a group, then you are only as free as they allow you to be. Freedom cannot be given by another.

**True leadership sets followers free
to be led by the Holy Spirit.**

True freedom is a product of truth, not legislation. It comes from the revelation of agitation. Jesus, expressing God's concept of freedom stated, "And you shall know the truth, and the truth shall make you free." In essence, he saw true freedom as a result of understanding the truth about yourself and everyone else. In other words, no one can give you the "right" to be free. Freedom is not something you receive, it is something that happens to you. Free men can never be bound.

The concept of freedom is concealed in the very word "freedom." This word is a grammatical construction of the words "free" and "dominion" and it comes from the concept of having the liberty to dominate. This truth is the very heart of the purpose for man's creation and is expressed in the very foundation of God's intention for mankind. In Genesis 1:26 he declared; "And let them rule over all the earth." This established not only the purpose for man's creation, but also the measure of his fulfillment.

In essence, no man is truly free until he has the liberty to dominate his environment, not other men. This is the heart of true leadership, to inspire men to declare independence from the bondage of other men's opinions and pre-judgements, and to tap the unlimited potential within them to creatively dominate the earth, which is his destiny.

Therefore, any leadership that restricts, denies, inhibits, limits, suppresses, oppresses, obstructs or frustrates this God-given mandate and capacity, is not leadership at all. True leadership sets followers free to be led by the Holy Spirit, for only him whom the Son sets free is truly free indeed.

"None of us is free until all of us are free."

LEADERSHIP CULTIVATION PROGRAM

Leaders learn by leading, because the only real laboratory is the laboratory of leadership itself. Leaders not only manage change, they must be comfortable with it in their own lives, and because we can all change then there is always room for improvement, refinement, cultivation and further development of our skills, character, knowledge and refinement of hidden talents and gifts.

Listed below are principles and precepts that must be present and developed if the leader is to deploy and maximize his full potential. Check Yourself against the following list and review it as your endeavor to incorporate each principle into your life and leadership.

1. I POSSESS A DEEP GUIDING PURPOSE

You must possess a deep guiding purpose, vision and a sense of destiny for your existence. You must know the meaningful significance for your life and have discovered the reason for your existence.

2. I HAVE A CLEAR VISION

You must have a personal and corporate vision. Just as no great painting has ever been created by a committee, no great vision has ever emerged from the head.

3. I LOVE TO SERVE OTHERS

You must live to serve others with a passion to see their lives improve and to maximize their potential.

4. I HAVE ESTABLISHED SPECIFIC GOALS

You must be goal oriented with documented, clearly defined personal and corporate goals that you intend to achieve.

5. I CULTIVATE MY SPIRITUAL RESERVES

You must have an intimate, personal relationship with your Creator and the Lord Jesus Christ. You must reserve regular times for solitude, prayer and meditation to replenish Spiritual Reserves.

6. I AM TEACHABLE

You must operate on the assumption that all I know is what I have learned and all I have learned is not all there is to know.

7. I AM CONSTANTLY REFINING MY SKILLS

You must constantly develop and refine your skills through an ongoing program of study, understanding that mastery and absolute competence is mandatory for a leader.

8. I AM TOLERANT

You must be patient allowing others to fail and grow understanding that potential is more valuable than behavior.

9. I AM HONEST AND SINCERE WITH INTEGRITY

You must maintain the highest standard of integrity honestly integrading your words, feelings, actions and thoughts into one complete whole.

10. I COMMUNICATE MY VISION

You must communicate your vision. What is to be done, who is to do it, and how it is to be done.

11. I AM AN AVID READER

You must read widely and deeply to cultivate the habit of sharpening your knowledge base. I keep up with current issues by reading the best literature, magazines, books, journals, etc.

12. I MAXIMIZE TIME

You must be deeply sensitive to the value of time and be meticulously careful in your selection of priorities.

13. I AM ENTHUSIASTIC TOWARD LIFE

You must radiate positive energy with an optimistic attitude and an enthusiastic spirit, full of Hope and Faith.

14. I BELIEVE IN THE WORTH AND VALUE OF OTHERS

You must believe in other people and appreciate their value and potential.

15. I KEEP MYSELF IN THE BEST CONDITION POSSIBLE

You must maintain a balance, moderate, regular program of exercise and proper diet to enhance your physical, mental, emotional and spiritual well being.

16. I EMBRACE RESPONSIBILITY CHEERFULLY

You must avoid procrastination and embrace active responsibility.

17. I AM DARING

You must initiate new ventures and welcome new ideas without fear of challenging convention and tradition.

18. I AM DECISIVE

You must make decisions and be fully aware of and accept the consequences of your decisions.

19. I AM RESULT ORIENTED

You must care more for the accomplishment of the task than who gets the credit.

20. I AM COMMITTED TO EXCELLENCE

You must give more than is expected of you and take pride in every task.

21. I LEARN FROM MY MISTAKES

You must learn from your mistakes and failures rather than allowing them to discourage, defeat or immobilize you.

22. I MEASURE MYSELF AGAINST MYSELF

You must measure your performance and success only against your potential and your purpose without comparing yourself or achievements with other people.

NOTE: "If you would be successful as a leader, discover what people want and help them achieve it." Your success comes when you are helping other people achieve what is important to them.

EXERCISE: Complete the following assignment as a personal commitment to enhancing your leadership edge: Take a blank sheet of paper and write your personal response.

My Purpose	-	Why I exist
My Vision	-	Where I intend to go
My Goals	-	What I intend to go
My Objectives	-	How I intend to do it
My Plan	-	Procedure
My Strategy	-	Co-Ordination of Resources

After you have completed this exercise, read this book again and commit to deploy the great leader within you.

I AM A LEADER

1. I POSSESS A DEEP GUIDING PURPOSE
2. I HAVE A CLEAR VISION
3. I LOVE TO SERVE OTHERS
4. I HAVE ESTABLISHED SPECIFIC GOALS
5. I CULTIVATE MY SPIRITUAL RESERVES
6. I AM TEACHABLE
7. I AM CONSTANTLY REFINING MY SKILLS
8. I AM TOLERANT
9. I AM HONEST AND SINCERE WITH INTEGRITY
10. I COMMUNICATE MY VISION
11. I AM AN AVID READER
12. I MAXIMIZE TIME
13. I AM ENTHUSIASTIC TOWARD LIFE
14. I BELIEVE IN THE WORTH AND VALUE OTHERS
15. I KEEP MYSELF IN THE BEST CONDITION POSSIBLE
16. I EMBRACE RESPONSIBILITY CAREFULLY
17. I AM DARING
18. I AM DECISIVE
19. I AM RESULT ORIENTED
20. I AM COMMITTED TO EXCELLENCE
21. I LEARN FROM MY MISTAKES
22. I MEASURE MYSELF AGAINST MYSELF

ABOUT THE AUTHOR

Dr. Myles Munroe is the multi-gifted International Motivational speaker, Author, Lecturer, Educator, Government Consultant, Advisor and Businessman, addressing critical issues affecting every aspect of Human, Social and Spiritual development. The central theme of his message is the discovery of Destiny, Purpose and The Maximization of individual potential.

He displays his multi-faceted ability to reach all aspects of the community by his many invitations to address the Religious, Business, Political, Civic and Educational communities in many nations. He is sought after by the leaders of various institutions and is currently serving as a consultant to a number of political leaders throughout the world. In 1991, He was selected and invited to the Round-Table committee to meet with the Government of Israel to contribute to the Middle-East Peace Talks.

He has traveled extensively throughout the United States, Canada, Central America, Europe, Africa, Israel, South America and the Caribbean as a conference Speaker, Seminar and Convention Teacher, Lecturer and Facilitator.

He has served as executive Assistant to the Bahamas Government Minister of Education and Administrative Assistant to the Permanent Secretary of Education. He further served as assistant Secretary to the Department of Public Personnel of the Government of the Bahamas. He presently holds the position of a consultant for Human Resource Development to the Government, and is a nationally respected leader in his nation.

He is also Founder and President of Bahamas Faith Ministries International, an all encompassing network of ministries with headquarters in Nassau, Bahamas. BFMI is also the Headquarters for the International Third World Development Center, a world-class Leadership Training Convention Center of which he is Chief executive Officer.

Dr. Munroe graduated from the Oral Roberts University in 1978 where he earned Bachelor of arts Degrees in Education, fine Arts and Theology. He went on to earn his M.A. Degree in Administration from the University of Tulsa, graduation in 1980. He is listed in numerous Biographical publications including Who's Who in American Universities and colleges.

In 1990, he was also chosen by the Board of Regents of Oral Roberts University to be the first ORU graduate in the University's 25 year history to give the Baccalaureate address at the University's graduation exercises. Also in May 1990, the Board of Regents conferred on him an Honorary Doctorate Degree from Oral Roberts University, which was presented by the President of the University, Dr. Oral Roberts.

Dr. Munroe is also the Lecturer and Teacher on "FAITH LIFE RADIO SEMINAR" and "FAITH LIFE" television program, both aired throughout the Bahamas and other Caribbean countries. He is also the principle host of "FRONTIER," a motivational series designed for Television and radio.

Dr. Munroe is also a frequent guest on numerous television and radio shows such as Trinity Broadcasting Network, Christian Broadcasting Network and other national programs.

Dr. Munroe says he is committed to communicating relevant, practical biblical principles in the simplest form so that every individual can comprehend and appropriate these principles and experience a better quality of life.

Myles and his wife Ruth are leaders with a sensitive heart, and ministers with an international vision. They are the proud parents of two children, Charisa and Myles Jr.

"Many are the plans in a man's heart but it is the Lord's purpose that will prevail."
Proverbs 19:21

189

BECOMING A LEADER:
Everyone Can Do It

Within each of us lies the potential to be an effective leader. **Becoming A Leader** uncovers the secrets of dynamic leadership that will turn your leadership potential into a potent reality. You will be encouraged and stimulated as you discover your natural leadership qualities lying dormant within you.

To order toll free call:
Pneuma Life Publishing
1-800-727-3218

OTHER BOOKS BY Dr. Myles Munroe:

Becoming A Leader	$9.95
Becoming A Leader Workbook	$7.95
How to Transform Your Ideas into Reality	$7.95
Single, Married, Separated and Life After Divorce	$7.95
Understanding Your Potential	$7.95
Understanding Your Potential Workbook	$6.00
Releasing Your Potential	$7.95
The Pursuit of Purpose	$7.95

OTHER BOOKS BY:

Dave Burrows, Youth Pastor, Bahamas Faith Ministries, Richard Pinder, Pastor, Bahamas Faith Ministries, Derwin Stewart and Dr. Mensa Otabil.

Strategies for Saving the Next Generation $5.95
by Dave Burrows

This book will teach you how to start and effectively operate a vibrant youth ministry. This book is filled with practical tips and insight gained over a number of years working with young people from the street to the parks to the church. Dave Burrows offers the reader vital information that will produce results if carefully considered and adapted. Excellent for Pastors and Youth Pastor as well as youth workers and those involved with youth ministry.

Talk to Me $5.95
by Dave Burrows

A guide for dialogue between parents and teens. This book focused on the life issues that face teens, ranging from drugs to sex to parents to music to peer pressure. This book will help both teenagers and parents gain a new understanding on these age old issues. Written "in your face" by a man who knows what it is to be a troubled youth living in a world of violence, drugs and street culture.

Mobilizing Human Resources $7.95
by Pastor Richard Pinder

Pastor Pinder gives an in-depth look at how to organize, motivate and deploy members of the body of Christ in a manner that produces maximum effect for your ministry. This book will assist you in organizing and motivating your 'troops' for effective and efficient ministry. It will also help the individual believer in recognizing their place in the body, using their God given abilities and talents to maximum effect.

The Minister's Topical Bible $14.95
by Derwin Stewart
The Minister's Topical Bible covers every aspect of the ministry providing quick and easy access to scriptures in a variety of ministry related topics. This handy reference tool can be effectively used in leadership training, counseling, teaching, sermon preparation and personal study.

Four Laws of Productivity $7.95
by Dr. Mensa Otabil
In Genesis 1:28, God commanded man to do four things: (1) "Be fruitful, and (2) multiply, and (3) replenish the earth, and (4) subdue it: and have dominion .." In the past, many people read and thought that this scripture only meant to have many children. This scriptural passage is not confined to reproduction, but is the foundation for all productivity. The Four Laws of Productivity by Dr. Mensa Otabil will show you how to: Discover God's gift in you, develop the gift, and how to be truly productive in life. The principles revealed in this timely book will radically change your life.

To order or to receive
a free brochure:

Call:
Bahamas Faith Ministries
1-809-393-7700
3362 NW 151st Terrace
Opa Locka, FL 33054

Or call:
Pneuma Life Publishing
1-800-727-3218
1-301-251-4470
P.O. Box 1127
Rockville, MD 20849-1127